QI FACTS SERIES

1,227 QI Facts To Blow Your Socks Off
1,339 QI Facts To Make Your Jaw Drop
1,411 QI Facts To Knock You Sideways
1,234 QI Facts To Leave You Speechless
1,342 QI Facts To Leave You Flabbergasted
1,423 QI Facts To Bowl You Over
2,024 QI Facts To Stop You In Your Tracks

GENERAL IGNORANCE SERIES

The Book of General Ignorance
The Second Book of General Ignorance
The Third Book of General Ignorance
The Book of Animal Ignorance
Advanced Banter: The QI Book of Quotations
The QI Book of The Dead

BY NO SUCH THING AS A FISH

The Book of the Year 2017
The Book of the Year 2018
The Book of the Year 2019

YOUR QUESTIONS ANSWERED BY THE QI ELVES

WITH A FOREWORD BY ZOE BALL

faber

BBC RADIO 2

First published in 2020
by Faber & Faber Ltd
Bloomsbury House
74–77 Great Russell Street
London WC1B 3DA
Published in the USA in 2020

Illustrations by Emily Jupitus
Design by Chris Shamwana
Typeset by Ian Bahrami
Printed and bound in England by CPI Group (UK) Ltd,
Croydon CR0 4YY

A CIP record for this book
is available from the British Library

ISBN 978–0–571–36337–7

FSC
www.fsc.org
MIX
Paper from
responsible sources
FSC® C020471

2 4 6 8 10 9 7 5 3 1

Foreword
by Zoe Ball

. . . .

In my day job I'm faced with a string of impossible questions. 'What's going on?' courtesy of Marvin Gaye. 'How will I know?' from Whitney Houston. 'Why do fools fall in love?' 'What's the frequency, Kenneth?' (and who on Earth is Kenneth?) 'What's new pussycat?' 'Is there life on Mars?'

Fortunately for my morning-addled self, I don't have to answer these – I just get to play the records. Although I am pretty sure that no one has found any life on Mars. Yet.

But it's not just the pop stars who are forever asking questions. All of us have this insatiable thirst for knowledge, whether about black holes (see page 212) or toilet rolls (see page 5). That's what inspired us to start the 'Why Workshop' segment on the BBC Radio 2 *Breakfast Show*. In amongst the songs, we wanted listeners to learn something from our little programme. And so, every week, we invite them to send us their latest ponderings and wonderings, no matter how big, small, silly or bizarre, and we satisfy them as best we can.

Well, technically *I* don't; that's where my crack team of barnstormingly brilliant QI Elves come in. Who better to answer our listeners' questions than the researchers behind QI, that fount of weird and wonderful information? Every week for the past 18 months they've chased down countless rabbit holes and always emerged not only with the answers, but with armfuls of extra facts and revelations. This book is bursting with the best of those, plus so much more that we never had time to discuss on air.

I always wish we had longer to talk to the Elves on the

radio. Every answer they give immediately spawns ten more questions that I want to ask. I've always been more of a questioner than an answerer. I was quite annoying at school, with my hand up all the time in class, wanting to ask just one more thing (until adolescence tricked me into thinking that chasing boys and painting my hair yellow was more urgent than interrogating my teachers). Still today, I find myself being sucked down information wormholes and spending hours hunting for answers to things I'm not remotely meant to be working on.

And now, as a parent, I've also got my kids asking me the impossible questions. That's why I love that many of the contributions in this book come from children – probably those same ones who are still putting their hands up, even after the bell rings. Now that I have a couple of my own I've realised that you can usually depend on them to ask the most thought-provoking – or infuriating, depending on how busy things are – questions. And when they're young they genuinely think you'll know the answers to all of them. It's a real perk of parenting. Not only does it give you a thrilling sense of power, but it also means that you actually have to go and discover the answers to make sure they keep believing in your all-knowing abilities for as long as possible. And it's finding out those answers that's the real treat.

That said, I must admit that sometimes I cheat when my kids' questions become too challenging, and I get my dad on the phone. He's built a career on making information accessible to children, so he's a secret weapon in that respect. He was always completely convinced that learning should never be something laborious or a duty, that it was meant to be fun. He instilled that in us kids from an early age, sometimes to the detriment of our schoolwork. A simple question about why $x = y$ when

I was stuck on my maths homework would result in hours of discussion, heading back to Archimedes supposedly leaping from his bath and shrieking, 'Eureka!' Fascinating, but not much help with my algebra.

It's those tangents that stick with you, though. Sometimes it's not the question itself, or even the immediate answer to it, but the unexpected directions it bounds off into that amaze you the most. A subject might not sound promising at the outset, but you're astonished by where it ends up. I guarantee you'll be astonished at where the answers take you. I don't know of another book that'll tell you about Michael Phelps's swimming race against a shark one minute (see page 88), the Guinness World Record for the most belly-button fluff the next (see page 144), and then go on to reveal the number that's the answer to life, the universe and everything (spoiler: it's not 42! See page 180).

Above all, this book is a chance to pause, sit back and marvel at our amazing world. Most of us lead such busy, frantic lives, and in any breaks we get we're blasted with news and facts and figures from all directions. It was either the Elves or my dad who told me that there's more information in one edition of the *New York Times* than the average person in the 17th century would have come across in a lifetime. And we barely allow ourselves to take a breath as we try to absorb it all. My recommendation is that whenever those day-to-day stresses start to overwhelm you, hit pause. Put down your phone or laptop. Turn off those news alerts and – don't tell my producer that I said this! – switch off the radio. Stop running around after the kids for five minutes, or worrying about work or what to make for dinner. Then pick up this book. Everything in here provides a blissful distraction from those daily anxieties, and a reminder of the extraordinary science, nature, history, humanity and everyday wonders that surround us.

And if you need another reason to read on, do it so that you can discover more questions of your own. Just like I do when I speak to the Elves each week, you'll come away with ten more questions for every answer you read, and that's a brilliant gift. It's because humans are so obsessively curious that they produced all the incredible ideas, inventions, art and technology that make our lives what they are today. We got to where we are because we kept on asking questions, so why stop now?

Let us introduce ourselves . . .

As the 18th-century philosopher Voltaire said, you should judge a person by their questions rather than their answers, and by that measure *The Zoe Ball Breakfast Show*'s listeners are nothing short of exceptional.

Every Wednesday since the 'Why Workshop' launched in January 2019, the QI Elves (who usually research and write for BBC Two's *QI*) have been let loose on BBC Radio 2 listeners' queries and tasked with finding the answers to conundrums such as 'Who alphabetised the alphabet?', 'Which fruit came first, the grape or the grapefruit?' and 'Duvets have "tog ratings", but what is a tog?'

This is the complete opposite of the way the Elves usually work. On *QI*, we look for an interesting answer *first*, and then try and find a question to fit it. Starting with the question takes longer because the minute you start looking into any subject, it immediately starts throwing up more questions.

For example, once we'd uncovered *why* 'squirrel-proof' bird food is covered in chilli, we immediately wanted to know why humans want to eat chilli in the first place. And once we investigated in which order to top a scone with jam and cream, we then wondered which is the 'correct' way to make your accompanying cuppa – tea first or milk first?

In this book you'll find our favourite questions posed by Radio 2's listeners, as well as the tangential questions and extraordinary facts that we uncovered along the way. There are also some brand-new questions where we took inspiration from the philosophical ('If aliens were watching Earth, what would they think of us?'), the playful ('Why does treading on

LEGO hurt so much?') and the everyday ('We don't have Coke, is Pepsi okay?').

We hope that by the end of this book your brain will be full of answers, but also buzzing with new questions as you spot even more occasions to ask 'Why?' And if you find one that you're stumped on, do send it our way. If Voltaire doesn't mind too much, then we are as happy to be judged by our answers as by our questions.

We hope you enjoy reading this book as much as we all enjoyed writing it.

Anne Miller, James Harkin
and James Rawson
Summer 2020

For more from the team behind QI, visit qi.com.
You can also follow the Elves on Instagram, Facebook and on QI's fact-filled Twitter account @qikipedia, and listen to their weekly podcast at nosuchthingasafish.com.

FUNNY YOU SHOULD ASK...

Can I dig a tunnel to the other side of the Earth?

It would need to be 8,000 miles long. That's almost a hundred times longer than the longest tunnel in the world today – the main water pipe under New York City. On the other hand, it's only about 20 times longer than the one China is pioneering at the moment – the Yunnan–Guizhou tunnel, which will bring water from the mountains to the desert and 'turn Xinjiang into California'.

The world's seven longest tunnels all carry water, not trains or cars, and none of them go straight downwards. If you want to do that, it's going to be rather tough.

The first issue is time. The deepest hole ever dug by human beings is the Kola Superdeep Borehole in north-west Russia. It's the end result of a project begun in 1965 to try and dig the deepest hole possible. It took the Soviet team 22 years to get 7.2 miles below the Earth's surface. If they'd been trying to get to the other side of the planet, they'd still have over 7,990 miles – and over a thousand years – to go. And also the Kola borehole is only nine inches wide, just enough to drop a football down it.

The next problem is the working conditions. Because the Earth is full of radioactive rocks, it gets very hot down there. The Kola borehole had to be abandoned when the temperature hit 180°C, as it was too high for the instruments to keep working. And the deeper you go, the hotter it gets. At the centre of the Earth, not only does the temperature reach 6,000°C, but the pressure is so intense it would feel like 50,000 elephants were standing on your head.

But let's say that, despite all this, you manage to build your tunnel. Where do you hope to end up? There's twice as much land in the Earth's northern hemisphere as in its southern hemisphere (and twice as much in the eastern as in the western one), which means it's tricky to find two bits of solid ground that can be connected by a straight tunnel passing through the middle of the Earth. If you started digging in the UK and went straight down, you wouldn't emerge in Australia but in the middle of the South Pacific.

A better place to start might be the Argentinian city of Formosa. It takes its name from *fermosa*, the old Spanish word for 'beautiful', and if you dug straight down from there, you'd reappear in Taiwan, which, by happy coincidence, used to be called Formosa, the Portuguese for 'beautiful'. Have a beautiful trip.

Deepest we've got

················· **BORING FACTS** ·····················

❭ The two giant boring machines that dug the tunnels for the extension of the London Underground's Northern Line were called Helen and Amy.

❭ The largest badger sett ever discovered had 50 underground chambers, 178 entrances and 879 metres of tunnels.

When does a sea become an ocean?

According to the US's National Ocean Service, there is only one ocean on the planet, and it's called the 'global ocean'. Historically, it has been divided into four smaller ones: the Pacific, Atlantic, Indian and Arctic.

Seas are generally smaller than oceans and almost always partially enclosed by land, but there are exceptions. The Sargasso Sea is a large body of water in the middle of the Atlantic with no land boundaries; instead, its borders are marked by the ocean currents around its edges. And sometimes bodies of water called 'seas' aren't actually seas at all: the Dead Sea and the Caspian Sea are both completely landlocked, which means they are actually lakes.

Currently, there is some confusion about whether or not the Southern Ocean, which surrounds Antarctica, counts as an official ocean alongside the Pacific, Atlantic, Indian and Arctic. The International Hydrographic Association recognised it as such in 1937, but it lost its status in 1953, due to countries arguing about its boundaries. It still hasn't been officially accepted back, even though almost all scientists agree that it's there.

Should the toilet paper hang over or under?

....

Over.

That's how it hangs in the original patent.

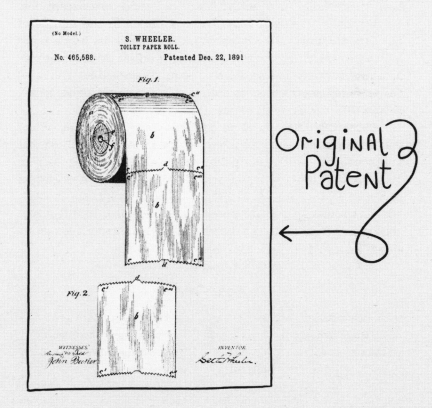

What is the worst misprint in history?

If you picked up *Webster's New International Dictionary* in 1934, you might have found this definition:

dord (dôrd), n. Physics & Chem. Density.

But 'dord' is not a physics and chemistry term for 'density'. The heading sent to editors was 'D or d', but somehow the letters got squashed into the single word 'dord'. For 13 years 'dord' sat in the dictionary between 'Dorcopsis' (a type of kangaroo) and 'doré' (gold-coated), until it was noticed and removed. It didn't magically become a word just because it was in the dictionary.

'Dord' may have been embarrassing for the writers involved, but it only cost them their pride. Others were not so lucky. In 1962, the unmanned NASA spacecraft Mariner 1 was due to fly close to Venus on an information-gathering mission. However, somebody made an error when the code for the navigation system was written, missing out a crucial line above the letter 'R'. This changed the rocket's course dramatically and instead of heading for Venus it went towards shipping lanes in the North Atlantic. NASA had no choice but to activate the self-destruct sequence less than five minutes

VeNUS

NOT VeNUS

after lift-off, costing them over $150 million in today's money.

Typos cost money, but they're also *on* money. In 2010, the Chilean mint produced thousands of 50-peso coins which spelt Chile 'C-H-I-I-E', and also spelt the end of the mint manager's career. Checking the writing on currency is a huge responsibility. Just ask the Australians who printed 46 million banknotes with the word 'responsibilty' on them.

Some mistakes might even have cost publishers their eternal souls. A 1944 edition of the Bible told women to submit to their 'owl' husbands instead of their 'own' husbands. In 1682, the so-called 'Cannibal's Bible' included the line 'if the latter husband ate her', instead of 'if the latter husband hate her'. Perhaps the most sinful mistake of all came from a 1631 edition, known as the 'Wicked Bible', which missed out the word 'not' in the Seventh Commandment, so it read: 'Thou shalt commit adultery.'

· **TPYO FACTS** ·

❯ When the French aristocrat Thomas de Mahy was shown his death warrant before being executed in 1790, his last words were: 'I see that you have made three spelling mistakes.'

❯ A typo that makes a different word that isn't picked up by a spellcheck (e.g. quite/quiet) is known as an 'atomic typo'.

❯ In a 2016 press release about the new English-language test for migrants, the British government misspelt the word 'language'.

Why aren't unicorns called unihorns?

The word 'unicorn' comes from the Romans, and they got it by combining the Latin words *uni* (meaning 'single') and *cornu* (meaning 'horn'). They couldn't use the word 'horn' because they didn't have it; English speakers got the word from old German tribes.

One of the earliest Western references to unicorns comes from a Greek historian who was seemingly fond of adding pointless 'c's to the start of his name. Ctesias of Cnidus lived around 400 BC and described unicorns as being the size of a horse, with purple heads, blue eyes and one single long horn. It's now thought that he was talking about a rhinoceros.

For a while people thought unicorns appeared in the Bible. There are references to a strong, horned animal called a 're'em', which has been translated as 'unicorn' or 'rhinoceros', but the current favoured interpretation is 'wild ox'.

Scientists are discovering new animals all the time, but it seems unlikely that we'll ever find a unicorn. Although as Lewis Carroll's unicorn said in *Alice's Adventures Through the Looking Glass*: 'Well, now that we have seen each other . . . if you'll believe in me, I'll believe in you.'

···················· **MYTH CONCEPTIONS** ····················

❯ The Danish throne was once thought to be made of unicorn horn. It is actually made of narwhal tusk.

❯ When notorious drug lord Pablo Escobar's daughter asked him for a unicorn, he had a horn stapled onto a horse's head.

If spiders can walk on the ceiling, why can't they get out of the bath?

Spiders are good climbers because of their hairy legs. Every individual hair is covered in hundreds of thousands of even more microscopic ones. And every hair that comes in contact with a surface creates a minute adhesive force. The more hairs that touch, the stronger the force.

On rough surfaces – like walls and ceilings – the lumps and bumps provide plenty of surface area for the hairs to touch. However, on very smooth surfaces, like the inside of a bath, fewer hairs can make contact, so the spider's grip is considerably weaker. This isn't a problem for small spiders, but larger ones are too heavy to pull themselves up without a rough surface to grab onto.

If you see a spider in your bath, it probably fell in while looking for something to drink. They don't climb up the plughole because modern drains contain a liquid-filled bend which is impossible for spiders to get past; equally, they can't use it as an escape route if they get stuck. So the simplest thing to do is to leave a towel hanging over the edge of the bath, and the spider will make its own way out eventually.

How much water would you need to put out the Sun?

In the first place, the Sun is not on fire. For fire to exist you need heat, fuel and oxygen – and there's no oxygen in space.

Like all the other stars in the sky, the Sun is just a giant ball of hot gas. It is so big that if the Earth were the size of the full stop at the end of this sentence, the Sun would be the size of a snooker ball. And because it's so large, the Sun has humongous gravity. If you could stand on its surface, you'd weigh as much as a hippopotamus.

The Sun's gravity creates astounding pressure. And the more pressure, the more heat. The temperature at the centre of the Sun is an unimaginable 15,000,000°C.

About 90% of the Sun is made of hydrogen, the simplest element in the universe. All this heat and pressure causes the hydrogen atoms to fuse together, forming atoms of the next simplest element, helium. This traumatic process is called 'nuclear fusion' and it gives off immense energy in the form of heat and light. Scientists have been trying to replicate hydrogen–helium fusion on Earth for decades. If they succeed, we will have an inexhaustible supply of clean green energy.

So what happens if you pour water on the Sun?

Essentially, all you're doing is adding to its mass, which increases its gravity and produces more fusion. This makes it even brighter and hotter. Worse still, water is two parts hydrogen to one part oxygen, so you're adding extra fuel to the mix too. Instead of putting the Sun out, the water will turn it into an even bigger star.

For any super-villain listening in and muttering, 'Curses! Foiled again!' there is one consolation: bigger and hotter stars tend to die more quickly than smaller ones, so sloshing loads of water over the Sun would shorten its lifespan, though it would take at least a million years before you would notice any change in size.

What would happen if the Sun died? Or if it was, in fact, put out by some evil genius? It would be a disaster, obviously, but it would take several days for enough heat to leak from the Earth that it would freeze. Your best bet for some kind of survival would be a home heated by a volcano or hidden at the bottom of the ocean, where thermal vents pump constant hot water. You'd have about a week to find one – in pitch darkness.

Interestingly, both of the above are places where super-villains traditionally hang out. Perhaps they know something we don't . . .

. . . .

Does the Sun make a sound?

Yes, but we can't hear it because space is a vacuum – it is completely empty – and sound can't travel if there's nothing for it to travel through. If you filled the Solar System with air, the sound from the Sun would be so deafening it would cause physical injury.

If aliens were watching Earth, what would they think of us?

Light is fast, but it still takes time to travel across the universe. So when you look at the stars in the night sky, you're seeing light that left those objects a long time ago. This means you're always looking into the past. If an alien living a hundred light years away turned on its television, even if your telescope was good enough you wouldn't be able to see the light from that TV screen for another hundred years. The same logic applies to anyone looking in the other direction. So what aliens think of us depends on how far away they are.

The nearest solar system to our own is Alpha Centauri, which is 4.37 light years away. Any aliens living there will be seeing the Earth as it was just over four years ago. So, at the time of writing, they are about to find out what happened in the 2016 EU referendum. Extraterrestrial beings who live close to Polaris (better known as the North Star) would be 434 light years away, so they might be watching Mary, Queen of Scots get arrested for agreeing to the assassination of her cousin Elizabeth I (alien spoiler alert: it doesn't end well for Mary).

Residents of Andromeda, our nearest big galaxy, would receive light that had left Earth 2.5 million years ago, so they might be watching *Homo habilis*, a species of ancient human that lived in Africa and used stone tools. To find aliens who can catch a glimpse of the dinosaurs you'll have to head out to a galaxy over 65 million light years away, such as the NGC 4845 galaxy in the Virgo system. But they'd need a hell of a telescope.

Why do dads make such bad jokes?

A 'dad joke' is different from a 'bad joke'. Or rather, it's a subcategory. It's a joke so terrible that it makes a child recoil in embarrassment, and only the dad finds it funny. It's also one that is repeated whenever the family is in a particular situation. And it's an affliction that almost all dads appear to suffer from.

There are a number of theories as to why dads make dad jokes. One is that when children are small, they will laugh at almost anything, even the inflection of their father's voice. So the dad thinks his bad jokes are funny, because they're getting laughs, and keeps on making them. When the child gets older, so (literally) do the jokes.

There's also a less insulting theory. Dad jokes are simple and rarely involve anything more than wordplay, so they can be useful in teaching language and social skills. The child's learning is increased because the jokes are repeated again and again.

Dad jokes exist all around the world. In Japan, they are called *oyaji gyagu*, or 'old man jokes', while the Korean word for the jokes, *ajae*, means 'middle-aged man'. In France, when a child says, '*Quoi?*' ('What?'), any self-respecting dad will reply, '*Feur*,' making the French word for 'hairdresser' – *coiffeur*. In Spain, if a dad sees any soy milk, he will respond with the classic '*Hola, Milk, soy Papi*' ('Hi, Milk, I'm Dad').

So next time your dad hears a police car go past and says, 'They won't sell any ice cream at that speed,' remember that you're not alone in your suffering.

Why did Hawaiians decide to put pineapple on a pizza?

They didn't – the Hawaiian pizza was invented by a Greek Canadian.

Pizza has a long and delicious history. The simplest version – a flatbread with various toppings – was eaten by the ancient Egyptians and Greeks, and from the very beginning they made them with fruit. 2,000 years ago, Virgil's *Aeneid* described the hero enjoying flatbreads topped with fruits from the forest, then commenting, 'See, we devour the plates on which we fed.'

The much-maligned Hawaiian pizza was invented by Greek restaurateur Sam Panopoulos. Having emigrated to Canada when he was 20, he ran a restaurant in Ontario with his brother, serving pizzas, burgers and Chinese food. In 1962, he mixed the sweet-and-savoury combinations found in Chinese cuisine with his ham-topped pizza to create the dish, which he named Hawaiian after the brand name on his tin of pineapple.

The topping has not been without its controversies. In 2017, Icelandic president Guðni Thorlacius Jóhannesson commented that he'd like to ban pineapples on pizzas – though he later added in an official statement: 'I do not have the power to make laws which forbid people to put pineapple on their pizza. I am glad that I do not hold such power.'

Why does my pizza taste so much better the next morning?

Pizza tastes great when it's cold. Cheese that's left out for a few hours becomes sweeter (as some of the milky lactose turns into fruity fructose), pepperoni becomes tastier (due to the proteins in the meat breaking down) and the garlic and herbs have more chance to infuse into the pizza. Crucially, the base stays crispy because the tomato sauce creates a barrier that doesn't let any additional moisture through.

It's even better news if you were drinking alcohol the night before, as your body starts to crave fatty foods thanks to a chemical called galanin, which is created in a hungover human's brain. Nobody's sure what exactly the point of galanin is, but we do know that when given to mice, it makes them want to eat fatty foods and drink more alcohol. The more they consume, the more galanin is produced and the more their cravings increase. It's a vicious (and delicious) circle.

KNEAD TO KNOW

> In 1950s Britain, pizza was promoted as 'Italian Welsh rarebit'.

> London's first pizzeria was a PizzaExpress. Customers were provided with plastic cutlery, but it was often melted by the hot cheese.

> Following a grant from NASA, a US company has developed 3D-printed pizza to feed astronauts.

> In 2017, an estimated 2,300 Americans had to visit the emergency room due to pizza-related injuries.

Why can't I order a
pint of wine in Britain?

The Great British pint can be traced back to Magna Carta, the foundation of the British legal system. The charter ruled (among many other things) that there should be 'one measure of ale, namely the London quarter'. The London quarter was the equivalent of two pints, and 800 years later it's still illegal in Britain to serve draught beer using any system of measurement other than the pint.

When the UK joined the European Community in 1973, it agreed to join the metric system, though it's fair to say that certain sectors dragged their feet. For wine, it was fairly straightforward as 99% of the wine drunk in Britain is (thankfully) imported. Most of that comes from Europe, where the metric system has been de rigueur since the 19th century. So, even in the mid-1800s, British landlords would buy their French Bordeaux and Spanish Rioja in litres, and it was easier to divide that into 125 or 175ml measures when serving punters rather than using imperial measurements.

Beer managed to escape metrification because in 1973 most of the beer drunk in Britain was also brewed there and had a long tradition of being served in pints. The EU spent three decades trying to persuade the UK to adapt, but in the face of staunch opposition, including from a pressure group called the 'Metric Martyrs', in 2007 it agreed that pints of beer could stay.

This means that while you can happily pour yourself a pint of wine or 250ml of ale to enjoy at home, in a pub, legally, it has to be the other way around.

Why do wine bottles have a dent at the bottom?

There is no agreement about why there's an indentation at the bottom of wine bottles, but there's no shortage of theories. The 'punt', as it is correctly called, comes with several advantages: an empty hidden space makes the bottle look like it contains more wine, which is useful for merchants; it also helps to catch the sediment, which is vital for drinkers; and it gives the pourer somewhere to put their thumb. But crucially, just as adding an arch to a bridge makes it stronger, adding a punt to a bottle gives it extra strength.

It was also important in the evolution of the champagne bottle. In the 1500s, French monks were making the world's first sparkling wine, but the increased pressure from the bubbles sometimes made the bottles explode. One exploding bottle would then disturb another, leading to a chain reaction that could destroy most of a cellar's stock. Being around sparkling wine was so dangerous that the French began to call it *le vin du diable* ('the devil's wine'), and brewers had to wear heavy iron masks to protect themselves. Bubbles were seen as a menace, and most winemakers did everything they could to keep their wine as still as possible. A solution was to come from an unlikely place.

In 1615, King James I was worried that Britain didn't have enough oak trees for building ships. To make sure that no timber went to waste, he banned the burning of wood in some industries, including glass-making. This meant that glassworkers used coal in their furnaces instead, which burns at a much higher temperature than wood, making much stronger glass. This new, sturdy material was perfect for bottling the French sparkling wine.

The new bottles were better, but accidents still happened. In 1826, German winemaker Georg Christian von Kessler entered his cellar to find that his entire year's output – 4,000 bottles – had smashed. He decided something needed to be done, and so approached local glassmakers Johann Georg Böhringer and Franz K. Klumpp, who took the thick English-style bottles and added a deep punt – and the modern champagne bottle was born.

. . . .

Why are large bottles of wine named after kings of Israel?
To ensure wine doesn't spoil, you need to limit the amount of air that comes into contact with it. Unfortunately, all bottles have a tiny bit of air between the wine and the cork, so in the 18th century vintners in Bordeaux began to make bigger bottles, which meant that less of the wine came into contact with the air, thus preventing it from going bad. The bottles were more expensive and named after Jeroboam, who was described in the Bible as 'a man of great worth'. When even bigger bottles were made, it was only natural to name them after other kings, such as Methuselah and Nebuchadnezzar.

. . . . **ABSOLUTE CORKERS** . . . .

❯ A glass of champagne contains about a million bubbles, each of which is a yeast micro-fart.

❯ It is estimated that Winston Churchill drank around 42,000 bottles of champagne in his life.

How do you grow seedless grapes?

If you cut a 'seedless' grape in half, you'll see that there *are* seeds in there, but they're so tiny and soft you don't notice when you eat them. And, actually, they don't function as seeds should.

You might suspect that without functioning seeds, the grapes must be grown in the lab, but in fact they've been grown since Roman times. As every gardener knows, planting seeds is only one way to grow plants. There's also 'grafting' (taking a bud or twig of one plant and lashing it to the cut part of another so that they heal together) or using 'cuttings', where a branch of a plant is cut off and stuck into the ground to begin a new one. Pretty much all apple trees are grown by grafting because, for some unknown reason, if you plant an apple seed, the tree that grows will produce apples that are completely different from the one that was planted.

Seedless grapes occasionally grow by chance, and when they do, new seedless plants can be cultivated using cuttings from those vines. They are rare in nature and result from a genetic mistake.

One of the most successful seedless grapes in history is the Sultanina from ancient Persia. In Australia and South Africa, it's known as the sultana grape, and in England as the Lady de Coverly. In 1872, William Thompson, a Scottish gardener who'd emigrated to the US, spotted some cuttings of Lady de Coverly in a New York nursery, took them out west and planted a tiny vineyard. After three years, he had managed to produce 50 lb of grapes.

Today, all US raisins are grown in California, and 95% of them are from those 'Thompson seedless' grapes.

Which is there more of in the world, custard or mustard?

The mustard family includes lettuce, cabbage, broccoli, kale, cauliflower, turnip, rapeseed, radish, Brussels sprouts, bok choi, wasabi, horseradish and more than 4,000 other species of plant.

The custard family includes only custard and crème anglaise, which is arguably just a fancy name for normal custard and is only ever used by people on TV cookery shows.

So we reckon the answer is mustard.

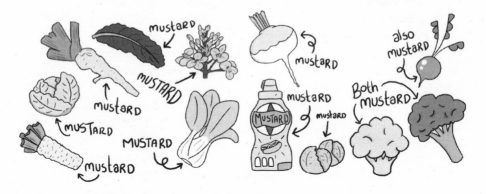

❯ The US's National Hot Dog and Sausage Council says it is not acceptable to put ketchup on your hot dog if you are over 18, but mustard is still allowed.

❯ If Heinz tomato ketchup pours out of the bottle unaided at a speed faster than 0.028 mph, it is rejected for sale.

Who was the first person to have a chip on their shoulder?

As you may know, in the US 'chips' are what we call crisps, and what we call chips are 'fries'. But this question has nothing to do with potatoes; it's about woodchips.

The first reference we could find to chips on shoulders comes from the British Royal Dockyards in the 18th century. It was a time when Britannia really did rule the waves, and during the reign of King George II (1727–60), the Royal Navy doubled in size. Vast numbers of trees were felled to be sawn up and turned into wooden battleships.

From 1739, one of the perks of the dockyard workers was to be able to take home offcuts of wood as fuel. The rule was that the 'chips' of wood could be no larger than could be carried on one shoulder. But, in 1753, the regulations were tightened up and the wood had to be carried under one arm. This was effectively a pay cut, and it led to a riot at Chatham Dockyard, with crowds of men pushing past the officers at the gates with blocks of wood on their shoulders in defiance of the order.

But we don't think that's where the expression comes from, because there's no record of the phrase 'having a chip on your shoulder' for another 60 years, when it surfaced in the US. Here, a tradition grew that punchy young men spoiling for a fight would strut around town with a chip of wood on their shoulder, daring people to try to knock it off. This practice is widely reported all over the US from 1817 onwards. It's also where we get the word 'chippy' from (as in 'he's a bit chippy'). You might think this is the origin of the phrase 'knock your block off' too, but it isn't. That's much older and dates back to 14th-century England. Hats used to be made using a block of wood as a mould, and so 'block' came to mean the thing your hat sits on, i.e. your head.

· ·

What about the phrase 'a chip off the old block'?

That's older still and dates back to ancient Greece. It used to be 'of the old block', rather than 'off', and refers to a boy who is recognisably a smaller version of his father, like a piece of stone chipped off a block when carving a statue.

· · · · · · · · · · · · · · · · · · **BLOCKBUSTING FACTS** · · · · · · · · · · · · · · · · · ·

❯ The sound of the Balrog in *The Lord of the Rings* was made by dragging a breeze block across a wooden floor.

❯ 'Mump' is a Devonshire word for a block of peat dug out by hand.

How much wood would a woodchuck chuck if a woodchuck could chuck wood?

The most concrete answer to this tongue-twister came from a wildlife expert named Richard Thomas at the New York Department of Environmental Conservation. In 1998, he was so fed up of people asking him this question that he decided to work out the answer.

Thomas calculated that when woodchucks – or groundhogs, as they're more commonly known – dig their homes, they move 300 kg of soil, so he figured that they could probably shift the same amount of wood. Though it would get tiring if they had to keep constantly redoing it . . .

How many leaves does an oak tree have?

Thankfully, you don't need to pluck all the leaves individually and count them because we know that, for a typical oak tree at least, the answer is 227,721 leaves . . . ish. That very specific number comes thanks to a team of mathematicians at the University of Washington who, in 2012, published a paper titled 'Branching Out: Modeling Leaf Weight by Tree Growth Simulation'.

Their calculations involved working out a tree's 'minimum twig length', 'trunk length' and 'average growth decay', as well as 'apical dominance', which describes how much thicker a trunk is than a branch, and how much thicker a branch is than a twig. The team applied their system to a mature oak and came up with the number 227,721, though they were at pains to point out that it was an estimate – albeit a highly educated one – and that the whole experiment 'proved to be a very difficult problem'.

So, if you're eyeing up a tree in your own garden, you could carry out your own bespoke calculation, but it's probably easiest to take their word for it that the average oak has somewhere between 200,000 and 500,000 leaves, and leaf it at that.

················· **AN UNBE-LEAF-ABLE FACT** ·················

❯ There's a species of spider in China that disguises itself so that it looks like a dead leaf when seen from below and a living one when seen from above.

Why are leaves green (and sometimes red or yellow) but not blue?

. . . .

Every day, the world's leaves produce six times more energy than the human race has consumed over the course of its entire existence. Powered by the Sun, they split the carbon dioxide in the air, absorbing carbon and pumping oxygen back out. In the process they combine the carbon with oxygen and hydrogen from water to make glucose, a kind of sugar that not only forms the cell walls of the plant, but is also the most important source of energy for life on Earth. This is the miracle called photosynthesis (Greek for 'putting together with light'), and life depends upon it. Leaves, to put it mildly, are quite interesting. But they are definitely not blue.

Nature is overwhelmingly green because plants absorb the Sun's light using a green pigment called chlorophyll. This means the plant takes in light from all the colours of the rainbow, except green, which it reflects back. In autumn, when leaves stop growing, the chlorophyll breaks down and allows other colours hidden in the plant – like yellow, gold and red – to show.

There are a few plants with non-green leaves. Some, like copper beech hedges, have red leaves all year round because they contain anthocyanin. Strangely, *anthocyanin* is Greek for 'dark blue flower'. Odder still, there are, in fact, no blue-pigmented flowers in nature. Delphiniums, cornflowers and forget-me-nots (and the tiny number of plants with blue leaves) only appear to be blue. It's an optical illusion, created by a kind of chemical trickery in which the plants use two different red pigments that react and create a molecule which reflects blue light.

Scientists are still working out why most leaves use chlorophyll for photosynthesis, as opposed to a different-coloured pigment. In 2020, one group suggested that the green part of the light spectrum is sometimes too intense for plants to deal with, and that's why they're green. But expect more explanations to come out in the coming years – one of the simplest questions you can possibly ask is still waiting for a totally definitive answer.

. . . .

Why is milk white when grass is green?
Grass is green because it contains chlorophyll, but cows can't digest chlorophyll, so most of it passes through the digestive system and reappears as a cowpat. For a cow, the useful parts of grass are its fibre and vitamins, which provide energy to create fats and proteins. Some of these fats and proteins then become the main constituents of milk, where they are responsible for its white colour.

If you're really sick of boring old white milk on your cornflakes, you can give it an orangey tint by feeding a cow a lot of carrots. The reddish chemical in carrots is called carotene, and cows can digest it much better than chlorophyll. What is definitely not true, though, is the belief that chocolate milk comes from brown cows. A 2017 survey by the Innovation Center for US Dairy found that 7% of Americans thought that was the case.

What's the point of snot?

The insides of your nose and throat are permanently lined with mucus. Even if you don't have a cold, your body contains enough mucus to cover a basketball court. It acts like a kind of flypaper, capturing any dust, smoke or bacteria you breathe in, and the whole lot slides harmlessly down your throat, keeping nasty stuff out of your lungs.

In the event that some of these unwanted particles get past your first defences, your body adopts plan B. Unfortunately, this is basically plan A in overdrive, the body working harder and harder to generate more and more mucus. A healthy person's mucus contains more than 95% water and is easy to make. Your body produces about three pints a day, extracting the necessary water from your blood.

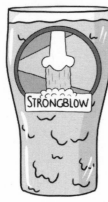

Human mucus contains powerful antibodies that attach themselves to bacteria and kill them. It also contains mucins. These are large molecules covered with sugar, which is what gives your snot that sticky consistency.

So next time you have a cold and are irritated by the vast amount of snot being produced, just be thankful it's working hard to return you to good health. And be grateful that while snot can be annoying, it doesn't define you. Unfortunately, the same cannot be said of a type of marine worm that lives at the bottom of the sea and eats the bones of dead whales. It's covered in mucus, which acts as a defence mechanism, and for that reason it's known as the bone-eating snot-flower.

· **SLIMY FACTS** ·

❯ Anything unwise enough to attack a hagfish gets glooped with five gallons of mucus, pumped out of 100 glands along their body. As a result, they have few predators.

❯ Snail mucus is used in skin creams.

Why do I find rain relaxing but a dripping tap infuriating?

Our brains interpret new noises as either threats or non-threats, so that we either jump in preparation for action or relax. Humans, like other mammals, are hard-wired to react to sudden sounds that come out of nowhere, even when they're not very loud, because they could mean bad news, from an insect sting to the threat of being hit by a car. They trigger a response from something called the 'threat-activated vigilance system'.

Watery sounds like the pitter-patter of rain or a babbling brook are non-threatening, so after a split second our brain allows us to drop our defences. The sound of rain can also act like a form of white noise, masking other noises that we would otherwise find irritating.

The sound of a dripping tap should theoretically provide the same level of relaxation as other watery sounds, but the problem comes from the gaps in-between. The first plop jolts you into defence mode, but by the time your brain has become used to it, another one falls, causing you to go back on high alert.

Interestingly, the sound of a tap dripping into a bucket isn't caused by the droplet hitting the water, but by a bubble of air forming under the drip as it hits the water surface. So you can put a stop to the sound by squirting some washing-up liquid into the water, which changes the surface tension and stops the bubble from forming. At least that will keep you sane until the plumber arrives.

Why does your brain often skip a repeated word in in a sentence?

Go back and and read that again.

And that.

Your brain is smart. Even when you're not thinking about it, you read sentences written in lower case MUCH QUICKER THAN THOSE IN UPPER CASE. Yuo cna aslo wrko out what a sneteecne says, even if some of the letters in the words are jumbled up. And it's vErY DifFiCuLt tO reAD words which contain a mix of upper- and lower-case letters. The reason for all this is that, when reading, we don't look at every letter individually, we scan the shape of the words.

If you watch someone while they're reading, you'll notice their eyes don't move smoothly; they make short, sharp motions known as 'saccades' (from the French for 'jerk'). When reading, you don't concentrate on every word. Luckily, your brain can usually work out what's coming next, and if it's confident, then it won't worry about the easy bits, like the three-letter words. These are often something like 'and' or 'the', and are unlikely to be particularly important to the story. In fact, this whole system works because about half the words in any sentence can be predicted from what has been written beanpole. Sorry, before.

················· YOU CAN SAY THAT AGAIN ··················

❱ When you repeat a word to clarify what you mean, such as 'going OUT out' or 'I LIKE like you,' this is known as contrastive focus reduplication.

Who alphabetised the alphabet?

The Phoenicians were an ancient civilisation who lived on the eastern coast of the Mediterranean around 1500–300 BC. They are remembered for their sea-faring, their fabulous purple dyes and for creating a system of communication that is the foundation of all modern alphabets.

Building on early writing that came from Egypt, the Phoenicians developed an alphabet in which every letter represented a single sound. This meant that letters could be grouped together to make any word or sentence that the writer could think of. Before this, symbols represented a whole word or syllable, so people had to memorise hundreds of characters if they wanted to read or write. Now they only had to learn 22.

Even though it was thousands of years ago, the resemblance between our alphabet and theirs is striking: the first four letters in theirs, Aleph, Bet, Gimel and Dalet, are early versions of 'A', 'B', 'C' and 'D'.

The simplicity of the Phoenician system, combined with their love of trade and travel, meant that their alphabet spread quickly across the Mediterranean region. The ancient Greeks adapted it and gave us the word 'alphabet', from their first two letters, alpha and beta. It continued to evolve until we arrived at the modern selection of letters that you're reading right now.

The ordering of the alphabet happened so long ago that we'll never really know who thought of it first. There are a few ideas, but they're just guesses. Some people think that the letters may have corresponded to numbers, so the alphabet is in numerical order. Others believe that the arrangement may have originally told a story or formed a sentence. There is also the possibility, of course, that it was just the random choice of A BC person.

. . . . ALPHABITS . . . .

❯ A person who is learning the alphabet is an 'abecedarian'.

❯ Louis Braille was just 15 years old when he developed the Braille alphabet. His system remains virtually unchanged today.

❯ Benjamin Franklin proposed to 'rearrange' the alphabet in the US, removing the letters 'C', 'J', 'Q', 'W', 'X' and 'Y'.

❯ An isogram is a word in which none of the letters are repeated. Some of the longest commonly used ones are 'dermatoglyphics', the study of skin markings, and 'uncopyrightable'.

What do Greek people say instead of 'It's all Greek to me'?

Είναι όλα ελληνικά για μένα

In Shakespeare's *Julius Caesar*, a Roman named Casca hears a speech that he doesn't understand and says, 'It was Greek to me.' It's one of the Bard's jokes: the speech would have been Greek to *everybody*, thanks to it actually being delivered in Greek. The saying didn't originate with Shakespeare; it probably dates back to medieval monks who understood Latin but not Greek. If they came across Greek in a manuscript, they would write in the margin: '*Graecum est; non legitur*' ('This is Greek; it can't be read').

The curious thing is that the phrase appears around the world, but with local variations. It's 'all Greek to me' in Dutch, Swedish, Norwegian, Portuguese and Spanish, but in Balkan countries they say, 'It's all Spanish to me.' In Bulgaria it's 'all Patagonian', in Finland it's 'all Hebrew', and in Greece they say, 'To me, this appears like Chinese.'

'It's all Chinese to me' also appears in Albania, Estonia, the Philippines and dozens of other countries. Of course, there's no such language as 'Chinese', as there are hundreds of languages spoken across China, but the two most important ones are Mandarin (the country's official language) and Cantonese. The Mandarin version of 'It's all Greek to me' is either 'This sounds like ghost's script' or 'This is the language of the birds,' while in Cantonese you'd say, 'This is like chicken intestines.' Much more fun.

> The French equivalent of 'the bee's knees' or 'the cat's pyjamas' is 'the baby Jesus with the velvet shorts!'

> *Moby Dick* has been translated into emoji.

> Instead of saying, 'It's raining cats and dogs,' the Welsh say, 'It's raining old ladies and sticks.'

> The Dutch phrase for 'urban legend' translates as 'monkey-sandwich story'.

What is the longest word?

The longest word in literature is '*lopadotemachoselachogaleokranioleipsanodrimhypotrimmatosilphioparaomelitokatakechymenokichlepikossyphophattoperisteralektryonoptekephalliokigklopeleiolagoiosiraiobaphetraganopterygon*', which was coined by the ancient Greek playwright Aristophanes. It features in his comedy *Assemblywomen*, from 391 BC, and is the name of a fictional meal made with dozens of ingredients, including fish, pigeon, crab and rotten dogfish.

There is a term that is too long to print in this book because it is 189,819 letters long and takes three and a half hours to read out loud. It's the full scientific name of a protein found in our muscles that is more commonly known as 'titin'. However, most dictionary compilers don't consider long chemical compounds to be 'words' as such, so don't go looking for it in your *Oxford English Dictionary*.

································· HAVE A WORD ·····················

❯ Pannapictagraphist – a collector of comic books.

❯ Brobdingnagian – enormous.

❯ Sesquipedalianism – the use of long or obscure words.

In 1896, what was the 937th most popular name for a baby boy in America?

Oddly specific question, but since you asked, it was Josephine.

❯ Using a middle initial in your name makes people think you are smarter.

❯ San Francisco's fog has a name: Karl.

❯ From 2002 to 2017, two satellites orbited the Earth, one chasing the other and carefully monitoring the distance between them. NASA nicknamed them Tom and Jerry.

❯ Over 3,500 children have been named after the *Game of Thrones* character Daenerys Targaryen.

❯ Children's names that have been blocked by judges in New Zealand include Yeah Detroit, Sex Fruit, Fat Boy, and Fish and Chips (for twins). The names Violence, Midnight Chardonnay and Number 16 Bus Shelter were all allowed.

❯ Four of the characters from *Frozen* – Hans, Kristoff, Anna and Sven – are named after Hans Christian Andersen, the author of the film's main inspiration, 'The Snow Queen'.

What did the ancient Egyptians call ancient Egypt?

The answer depends on which ancient Egyptians you ask, as Egyptian civilisation spanned three millennia and its people spoke five different languages, one after the other. These are now named Archaic Egyptian, Old Egyptian, Middle Egyptian, Late Egyptian and Demotic ('of the people') Egyptian. Inevitably, over this period they developed many different ways of referring to their land:

*Black Land (*kemet*) and Red Land (*deshret*)*
Kemet (probably pronounced 'kermit') represented the dark, fertile soil around the Nile. *Deshret* was the dry, desert region on either side. Because the fertile part was richer, more populous and more important, *kemet* came to refer to the whole of Egypt.

*The Top (*ta-shemau*) and the Bottom (*ta-mehu*)*
The Top referred to what looks like the bottom of Egypt on a modern map – the south – and the Bottom referred to the top – the north. Even today, Upper Egypt is the south and Lower Egypt is the north. It's another reference to the Nile: the south of the country is *up*river and the north is *down*river.

The Sedge and Bee (nesut-bity)

The grass-like sedge plant represented Upper Egypt, and the bee was the emblem of Lower Egypt. Rulers were often called 'He/She of the Sedge and Bee'.

Two Lands (ta-wy)

Pharaohs were sometimes also called 'Lords of Two Lands'. They wore a 'double crown', with the front half symbolising Upper Egypt and the back half symbolising Lower Egypt.

The most important city in ancient Egypt was Memphis, which Egyptians knew as the 'House of the Spirit of Ptah' (*hwt-ka-Ptah*). Ptah was the god of craftsmen and architects, and this is where the word 'Egypt' comes from. When the Greeks arrived in the 4th century BC, they mispronounced *hwt-ka-Ptah* as 'aeguptos', and over the centuries this has become 'Egypt'.

What was Ethelred the Unready not ready for?

A thousand years of people misunderstanding his nickname.

Ethelred ruled England from 978–1013 and again from 1014–16, and he wasn't very good at it. From 980, Danish Vikings regularly raided English shores, and Ethelred's response was twofold. The first was to pay the Danes enormous amounts of money to stay away; and when that didn't work, the second was to massacre any Danish settlers. Neither approach was a success, and he even lost his throne to Denmark's Sweyn Forkbeard (hence the gap in his reign), only getting it back because Sweyn died.

It was 150 years after Ethelred died that he was first called 'Unready' or 'Unread'. But the word, from the Anglo-Saxon *unraed*, didn't mean what it does today. *Raed* was 'counsel' or 'advice'; *unraed* was 'no counsel' or 'bad counsel'. With hindsight, it was obvious to anyone that the King had been either badly advised or not at all, hence the nickname. As the 'red' in Ethelred also comes from *raed* and *ethel* is Old English for 'noble', Ethelred translates as 'Noble Counsel'. So Ethelred Unread is actually meant as a joke: it translates as 'Noble-Counsel No-Counsel'.

Ethelred wasn't the only aristocrat cursed with an unfortunate nickname. Alfonso the Slobberer became king of León and Galicia in the 12th century, Childeric the Idiot was the last Merovingian ruler of the Franks, and the less said about the Norse king Eystein the Fart, the better.

Why don't we have royal nicknames any more?

After the Norman Conquest, we started numbering our kings and queens instead of nicknaming them. William I, better known as William the Conqueror (or as William the Bastard in Normandy), is the last English monarch to be remembered by his nickname. Each one since has just had a number. This should have made everything simpler for historians, but as nobody had bothered to number the kings before 1066, it wasn't. So the king who ruled from 1272 to 1307 is known as Edward I, even though there were three King Edwards before him. You could argue he was really Edward IV and that Edward VIII should be called Edward XI.

Things were further complicated when James VI of Scotland was invited to rule England, which had never had a King James before. So the English called him James I, but the Scots went on calling him James VI. His grandson became both James II and James VII. In 1953, to avoid similar confusion in the future, Winston Churchill decided that the higher number, whether used in Scotland or England, should be adopted everywhere. This means that if there's another King James, he will be James VIII, even though England has never had a King James III, IV, V, VI or VII.

Is any other country more confused about their royal numbers than Britain?

The entire Swedish system is pretty dubious, as 16th-century brothers King Erik XIV and King Charles IX numbered themselves after reading a grand history of Swedish kings. Unfortunately, the book they read was largely fictional and most of the Eriks and Charleses were made up. But Erik XIV and Charles IX liked the big numbers because it made them sound more impressive.

Which ruler had the highest number?

That honour surely belongs to Heinrich LXXII (72nd), Prince Reuss of Lobenstein and Ebersdorf, who ruled over an area of east Germany from 1822 to 1848. His family had an unusual system in that every male was called Heinrich, and each Heinrich received a number, whether they became ruler or not. Every hundred years the system was reset, starting again at Heinrich I.

········· CROWN JEWELS ·········

❯ Jadwiga was the first female monarch of Poland. She held the title of king because queens couldn't rule, but the law didn't state that a king had to be male.

❯ King Ragnar Hairy Breeches got his epithet due to the hairy trousers his wife made for him from animal skins.

Why are people who don't drink alcohol referred to as being teetotal?

It comes from the north-west, via the Wild West.

In 19th-century America, people in the Wild West were creating their own slang. While many of the words, such as 'obflisticated' (meaning 'flustered') and 'bodyaciously' (meaning 'completely'), are sadly no longer used today, there was another: 'tetotaciously', which lingered a little longer.

'Tetotaciously' meant 'totally'. In fact, it meant more than that. By stressing the initial 't', it implied something that was 'absolutely, completely, total'. The word was shortened slightly to 'tetotal', and it spread, first to the Irish population of North America, and eventually to the working class in the north of England. At a temperance meeting in Preston in 1833, a reformed boozehound named Richard Turner announced in a speech: 'I'll have nowt to do with the moderation botheration pledge; I'll be reet down T-total, that or nowt!' It was exactly the catchy phrase that the abstinence movement needed, and it's never had anything to do with cups of tea.

················· HAVE I GOT BOOZE FOR YOU ··················

❯ A study published in the *Medical Journal of Australia* called 'Licence to Swill' found that James Bond has a 'severe alcohol use disorder'.

❯ Dwarf hamsters can, proportionally, drink ten times as much alcohol as humans without displaying any signs of drunkenness.

In medieval times, when castles were attacked with catapults, where did they get all the rocks from?

Genghis Khan catapulted to fame in the 13th century, when he and his Mongol army invaded and conquered much of Europe and Asia with their tactics of besieging cities and massacring civilians. His empire stretched from the Sea of Japan in the east to the mountains of Austria in the west, but as anyone running a quickly expanding business will tell you, optimal functionality over long distances comes with certain operational issues.

The first problem for the Mongols was how to get their war machines to the site of the battle. 13th-century catapults were large and unwieldy weapons. Any attempt to make them more portable would also have made them less effective, so Genghis made engineers a permanent part of his army and would construct his weapons on site. He also offered huge rewards to enemy engineers who agreed to defect to the Mongol side.

But even the best team needs material to work with. At that time in Europe, soldiers would load catapults with whatever was lying around the walls of the city. Once the large rocks had run out, they might fire lots of smaller stones, before resorting to dead animals or piles of rubbish. But the Mongols never ran out of grade-A ammunition.

When the rulers of one Chinese city heard that the Mongol army was on its way, they came up with a novel defence and sent people to collect all the rocks from the nearby fields. Over days they removed every piece of stone for miles around, in the hope that the invaders wouldn't find anything to fire at their city. But the Mongols chopped down the local mulberry trees, soaked the trunks in water and left them to harden in the sun, giving them hundreds of wooden projectiles that were almost as hard as stone.

If stones were scarce and a city's walls too strong for hardwood, Genghis had a second contingency plan. Whenever the Mongols found a particularly rocky area, they would collect as many stones as possible. They then set up depots to store them, each a single day's ride from the last one. This meant that they had a never-ending reserve of rocks, and it was only a matter of time before the enemy would be beaten, defeated by both a brutal army and a brutally efficient supply chain.

Why is there an Essex, a Wessex and a Sussex, but no Nossex?

When the Romans left Britain in around AD 400, the islands were extremely susceptible to invasion. Numerous groups arrived from Europe, settled in different regions and started naming these areas after themselves.

The biggest of these was the Saxons, a group who came from modern-day Germany and the Netherlands. They're responsible for the 'sex' in Essex, which was where the East Saxons settled, Sussex, where the South Saxons lived, and Wessex (which covered much of the south coast from Hampshire to Devon), where you could find the West Saxons.

There was no Nossex because the Saxons didn't get particularly far north. The Angles had come over from Denmark and made their home up there. Then there were the Jutes, who came from another part of Denmark and settled in Kent, Northumbria (the lands 'North of the Humber') and Mercia, which got its name from a word meaning 'boundary lands'.

Wessex, Essex, Sussex, Anglia, Kent, Northumbria and Mercia are often described as the 'Seven Kingdoms', and George R. R. Martin was partly inspired by these divisions for his *A Song of Ice and Fire* books, on which the TV series *Game of Thrones* is based, but medieval Britain was actually much more complicated than that. Smaller kingdoms included Deira, Dumnonia, Haestingas, Hwicce, Magonsæte, Tomsæte, Wreocensæte, Wihtwara and Lindsey.

Do flamingos really produce milk, even though they are birds?

Surprisingly enough, they do, but it's not exactly the same as the milk made by mammals.

Flamingos are wading birds. When they're hungry, they use their feet to disturb the water and kick up tiny crustaceans and algae. Next they bend down and suck in water through their beaks, before forcing it back out through a special filter that catches pieces of food, which can then be eaten.

Baby flamingos' tiny beaks don't have a filter as this takes several weeks to develop. In the meantime, they can only manage a liquid diet, so the adults have to provide them with a milk-like substance containing all the protein and nutrients they need. Flamingo milk is made in glands that line the bird's throat (which means both males and females can make it), and since birds don't have nipples like mammals, the flamingos feed it to their chicks from their beak.

There are natural chemicals in a flamingo's diet of algae and shrimp that build up in their bodies and are responsible for them being pink. These chemicals end up in their milk, which as a result is bright red. Over the two months the babies rely on the milk, they become pinker and pinker, while the parents become paler and paler as they are literally drained by their children.

······················ FACTOSE INTOLERANCE ····················

❯ Tsetse flies, spiders and sharks all make milk.

❯ Pigeons and penguins also produce milk, but theirs is thick like cottage cheese.

How do you build a crane?

If you've ever walked past a building site and tilted your neck back to look at the top of a crane, you might have imagined it was built by an even bigger crane, which was in turn made by an even taller one – like a never-ending set of nesting dolls. However, most cranes build themselves.

A crane is made of a cabin, a base and a long tower in-between. The tower is made of lots of identical sections that lock together, along with a special piece called the 'climbing frame'. This frame, which is slightly wider than the rest of the tower, can push all the sections above it upwards, creating a gap where a new section can be slotted in. The process is repeated over and over until the crane reaches the required height.

Once completed, the cabin is a long way from the ground, so it needs to be accessed via a ladder inside the tower. And once you're up there it's a long way down, especially if you need to use the toilet, so crane operators tend to take a bottle up with them. A urinating crane driver in China got into trouble in 2019, when a gust of wind blew his wee out of the cabin. Someone had looked up to see what was happening, and it landed in their mouth. So next time you're admiring a crane, maybe don't get too close.

· TALL TALES ·

❯ The world's tallest land-based crane is 250 metres tall, can lift the equivalent of 1,600 cars at once and is called 'Big Carl'.

❯ Cranes are the world's tallest flying birds, reaching up to 6'6" in height.

If you can be underwhelmed and overwhelmed, can you ever just be whelmed?

The word 'whelmed' is older than both the under- and over-versions. It was first used 700 years ago, when it meant 'overturned' or 'capsized', before evolving to mean 'buried', 'submerged' or 'ruined'. 'Whelmed' appears in Chaucer's *Troilus and Criseyde*, Shakespeare's *The Merry Wives of Windsor* and John Milton's *Paradise Lost*, which includes the line 'One blow unaided could have finisht thee, and whelmd thy legions under darkness.'

'Overwhelmed' appeared a hundred years later. It took on a similar meaning – 'to be submerged' or 'overpowered' – and 'whelmed' largely dropped out of use.

'Underwhelmed' is a much more recent invention. It was first used in the 1950s, giving it the most underwhelming history of the three by far.

Why are the hottest days of the year in July and August, when the longest day is in June?

Today's temperature is not just determined by how much heat has come from the Sun since it rose this morning, but also by how warm it has been in recent days. Heat that has been absorbed in the ground and ocean can slowly escape over subsequent days and warm up the air. And if the ground isn't as hot as the air, it will suck in warmth from the atmosphere.

Although we get more hours of sunshine in June, the ground hasn't finished warming up yet. By late July or early August, it's hot enough to reach a balance with the heat of the atmosphere, so it stops taking in so much of the Sun's energy. That's when we get our highest temperatures. This delay between the longest day and the hottest day is known as 'seasonal lag'.

The rate of lag varies around the world, depending on local geography. Because the land heats up more quickly than the ocean, somewhere with lots of land and not much water will have its hottest day quite soon after its longest day. On the other hand, somewhere near a lot of water will have its hottest day a long time after its longest day. For instance, in San Francisco, which is surrounded by water on three sides, the hottest month is September.

Seasonal lag happens in winter too. Just as the ground takes a while to heat up, it takes a while to cool down. The shortest day in the UK is 21 December, but the coldest days are usually much later. To take a recent example, the lowest temperature of the 2018/19 English winter was recorded during the early hours of 3 February. Appropriately, it was reached in a remote part of Northumberland called Chillingham Barns.

· ·

Can animals get sunburnt?

They can. Newly shorn sheep and recently clipped animals are at particular risk. As are animals without fur, such as pigs and rhinos, who cover themselves with mud to protect against sunburn. Hippos take things one step further and secrete their own natural sunscreen. This red, oily, sweat-like substance contains not only microscopic structures that scatter light and protect their skin, but also antibiotics, and it acts as a moisturiser.

· · · · · · · · · · · · · · · · · · · **A LITTLE SEASONING** · · · · · · · · · · · · · · · · · · ·

❯ On 28 June 2018, it was thought that a new record had been set for the hottest temperature ever measured in Scotland. However, the record had to be rejected when it was discovered that the thermometer had been placed next to the exhaust pipe of a car that had its engine running.

❯ Ancient Japan had 24 seasons and 72 microseasons, including 'caterpillars become butterflies', 'plums turn yellow' and 'rainbows hide'.

What is the highest-scoring move in Scrabble?

Like many Americans, Alfred Butts, an architect by trade, found himself unemployed during the Great Depression and had to think of an innovative way to make money. As crosswords, number games and board games were popular at the time, he set to work on making something that would combine all three. Having decided on the idea for the game he called Scrabble, he spent months painstakingly reading the front page of *The New York Times*, counting how often each of the alphabet's 26 letters appeared. He used his final tally to decide on how many tiles of each letter should go into a Scrabble set.

When the game went on sale in the 1940s, it wasn't a huge success. The turning point came in 1952, when the president of Macy's department store found a set while he was on holiday in Florida and became a fan. When the famous shop started stocking Scrabble, it was soon selling 6,000 copies a week. Today, over 150 million sets have been sold worldwide, and around 30,000 games are started every hour.

The highest-scoring Scrabble move on record was played by Manchester's Dr Karl Khoshnaw at a tournament in 1982. He spelt out 'CAZIQUES', and it bagged him 392 points. 'Cazique' is another word for the American oriole bird.

'CAZIQUES' isn't the highest-scoring word possible, though. In theory, 'OXYPHENBUTAZONE', a type of anti-inflammatory drug, could get you 1,780 points, if it was played on a board that had the letters already set up in the right way. However, the chances of that board coming up during normal gameplay are astronomically small. Incidentally, while 'OXYPHENBUTAZONE' may be among the least common words played in Scrabble, the most common – in competitions at least – is 'QI'.

· · · · · · · · · · · · · · · · · · TRIPLE NERD SCORE · · · · · · · · · · · · · · · · · · ·

> In Armenia, players have created a 17 × 17 board instead of the usual 15 × 15 layout because their words are so long.

> Another unofficial game is 'Maths Scrabble', where instead of a word you have to put down a mathematically correct equation.

Where did the alphabet song come from?

In 1835, an American composer called Charles Bradlee wrote a song called 'The ABC, a German air with variations for the flute with an easy accompaniment for the piano forte'. The tune was the one we now use for 'Twinkle, Twinkle, Little Star', and the lyrics were little more than the letters of the alphabet, but Bradlee was still awarded the copyright and managed to profit from his 'composition'.

The lyrics for 'Twinkle, Twinkle, Little Star' date back to the early 1800s, but the melody is much older. It comes from a French folk song called 'Ah! vous dirai-je, Maman' (which translates as 'Ah! Shall I tell you, mother?'), and it was made popular by none other than Wolfgang Amadeus Mozart, who composed twelve variations on the theme when he lived in France in his 20s. It is also the tune of 'Baa, Baa, Black Sheep'.

One of the problems with Bradlee's alphabet song is that the 'L, M, N, O, P' bit is quite fast, making it difficult for children to pronounce each letter individually. In 2010, a remixed version appeared on YouTube, where the letters 'L', 'M' and 'N' are sung at the same speed as the start of the song. You then take a breath before stringing together 'O, P, Q, R, S, T, U', then singing 'V' on its own, before finishing with 'W, X, Y and Z.' It's had nearly 11 million views, though opinion on whether it is a stroke of genius or the worst thing ever to have been posted on the Internet is somewhat divided.

Not only does the way children recite the alphabet constantly change, but the alphabet itself has changed over the years. A few of the characters that we've lost from English over the last thousand years include eth (ð), thorn (þ), wynn (ρ), yogh (ʒ), ash (æ) and our favourite, ethel (œ). In 19th-century America, it was taught that the '&' symbol (meaning 'and') was the 27th letter after 'Z'. When children recited the alphabet, they would finish with 'X, Y, Z and per se and', with 'per se' meaning 'by itself'. This phrase was eventually shortened to 'ampersand', the symbol's modern name.

. . . .

Since there are so few musical notes, will there come a time when we run out of new combinations and are no longer able to create new tunes?
In Western music there are twelve notes (A, B, C, D, E, F and G, plus sharps and flats). Working in different combinations, these have given us everything from Beethoven to Beyoncé.

If a musical ditty has a sequence of just 20 notes, then the number of possible combinations is already 35 billion times greater than the number of people who have ever lived. And that's to say nothing of note length, volume, tempo, instrument, and the fact that not all music uses this Western scale.

Over the centuries, composers have found ways to be creative with the notes available. The serialism movement used all 12 notes to create musical phrases, while minimalism took short phrases which were then repeated over and over. Aleatory music (taken from the Latin *alea*, meaning dice) left some elements to chance, whether that was a loose directive like 'play for five minutes' or choosing the next notes based on the roll of a dice.

Some composers have done away with notes altogether, as in John Cage's 'silent' '4'33"', in which performers don't play their instruments for the duration of the piece.

Because chess has been played so many times over the centuries, has every possible game, move for move, already been played before?

. . . .

No.

There are more possible games of chess than there have been seconds since the start of the universe. And no one is that quick at chess.

What is the origin of the phrase 'sent to Coventry'?

Being 'sent to Coventry' is a popular punishment in Enid Blyton's boarding-school series *Malory Towers*. If someone did something to displease the class, they would respond by sending the offending pupil to Coventry – meaning no one would speak to them until the punishment ended.

There are several theories about the idiom's origin, and all are much grimmer than midnight feasts and playing pranks on teachers. One comes from the English Civil War, when Oliver Cromwell's troops captured a group of Royalist soldiers and held them in a church in Coventry. Most of the locals were on Cromwell's side and didn't like the idea of lots of soldiers coming to their town and causing a nuisance. As a result, they shunned the Royalists, and the idiom was born.

An even darker theory is that during the reign of Henry III, traitors were on occasion hanged from a covin tree (a Scottish word for a tree outside a mansion beneath which visitors would be met), and so being sent there was a euphemism for execution. It has also been suggested that it refers to Peeping Tom, who supposedly spied on Lady Godiva when she rode naked through Coventry to protest against taxes. Depending on who is telling the story, Tom was punished by being either blinded or killed. But given that getting 'sent to Coventry' is about being shunned rather than murdered, we can probably discount both of these explanations.

Why does treading on LEGO hurt so much?

It's a sore point.

LEGO bricks are made with an ultra-hard plastic that can withstand a force equivalent to having a grand piano dropped on top of them. This gives them a long lifespan, but it also means that, unless you weigh more than a grand piano, they stay solid if you step on them. All the pressure created by your weight is absorbed by your foot as you walk. It's the exact opposite of the bed of nails trick, where lying on upturned spikes doesn't hurt so much because the body's weight is spread out over a large number of individual points.

But it's not just LEGO that's to blame for the pain of standing on a brick; it's also the way our feet have evolved. Our soles are one of the most sensitive parts of our bodies, with over 7,000 nerve endings in each foot. If your feet are injured, then it severely impairs your ability to function, so the body needs to warn you very quickly if something's wrong. That's a good thing if you're a hunter-gatherer on the plains of Africa, but not much help if you're in a toddler's bedroom in your pyjamas. People who walk on hot coals and broken glass for a living say that stepping on LEGO is far, far worse.

LEGO was invented by a Danish master carpenter called Ole Kirk Kristiansen. At first, the bricks were made of wood, but things really took off after he bought the first plastic moulding machine in Denmark. He offered his seven staff a prize of a bottle of home-made wine if they could come up with a name for the product. In the end, he chose his own suggestion, LEGO, short for the Danish *leg godt*, meaning 'play well'.

Lego is Latin for 'I collect', but, rather pleasingly, it also means 'to remove fragments surgically'.

· **LEGO FACTS** ·

❯ LEGO is the world's largest manufacturer of vehicle tyres.

❯ It takes an average of 1.71 days for the head of a LEGO figure to pass through a human's digestive system.

Who popularised the recorder, and where can I get my hands on them?

During the Renaissance period, the recorder was the instrument of choice for upper-class gentlemen who wanted to practise music but hoped to do so quietly. They were expected to become skilled players, but not quite up to the standard of professional musicians, who were of a lower class. If someone became too good, there would be a suspicion that they were spending too much time on the recorder and not enough on other gentlemanly pursuits.

After the Renaissance came what's now known as the Baroque period, during which musicians such as J. S. Bach, Henry Purcell and Antonio Vivaldi all embraced the recorder to replicate birdsong or suggest other countryside activities. The instrument's popularity can also be seen in the art world: there are more than a hundred Dutch works from this time that show a recorder either being played or as part of a still-life painting.

The Classical era of Mozart and Beethoven brought with it larger orchestral pieces. Amid such a grand collection of instruments, the breathy, high-pitched recorder was lost. So composers stopped writing for it, and the recorder returned to its place as a practice instrument for wealthy families.

But that all changed in the first half of the 20th century, thanks to German composer Carl Orff. His *Schulwerk* was a lifelong project that he hoped would teach children the basics of musical knowledge. It featured the recorder heavily. The instrument was cheap, simple to manufacture and fantastically easy to play. It can be hard to get any noise from many other instruments, but with this one it's simple: get recorder, hold recorder, blow.

Carl died in 1982 and was buried in a Bavarian church in a place called Andechs, so if you want to find the final resting place of the man responsible for all those nightmarish children's concerts, you're best heading Orff to south-east Germany.

· ·

Why is my singing voice different from my speaking voice?
There are two main differences between speaking and singing. The first is that singing uses more lung pressure; the second is that the gaps above your vocal cords open up when singing, allowing the sound to resonate. These two changes mean that when you sing, your vowels become much longer, and so you sing in a slightly different accent. For English people, having longer vowels tends to make them sound more American.

· · · · · · · · · · · · · · · · · · · **RECORDED FACTS** ·

❯ In 2005, a 14th-century recorder was discovered in an Estonian toilet.

❯ The recorder's name comes from the medieval minstrels who would learn (record) and recite poetry as part of their repertoire, often accompanied by music.

Who is the most isolated person in the world?

. . . .

The Amazon rainforest is home to more than 2 million species of animal and almost 400 billion trees, but you could walk for a long time before coming across evidence of another human. One area, the Vale do Javari, is so unexplored that Brazil's highest mountain remained undiscovered there until 1962. There are tribes who live in Brazil's wilderness, out of contact with the modern world, and one of them is down to a single member.

Brazilian officials first became aware of the man's existence around 25 years ago and gave him the nickname 'Man of the Hole', due to the fact that he builds temporary homes which all have a large hole dug alongside them. Nobody is quite sure what the holes are for: they might be to capture animals to eat, or to hide in, or they could have religious significance. The only way to know for sure would be to ask him, but that's impossible: the Brazilian government has declared that an area of 31 square miles surrounding him is off-limits to anyone else. It's part of their 'policy of no contact', the idea being that if uncontacted tribes want to reach out, then they should be able to do so on their own terms rather than having the modern world forced upon them. As such, even though he is often described as 'the loneliest person in the world', we don't know that the Man of the Hole feels lonely, only that he is alone. He may like it that way.

In 1969, a contender for loneliest person in the Solar System was astronaut Michael Collins. When Neil Armstrong and Buzz Aldrin first set foot on the Moon, the whole world was watching. The whole world, that is, apart from Collins, who was circling around the back of the Moon, looking after the command module. When he was fully behind it, mission control couldn't get messages to him, so Collins was literally on his own, temporarily separated from every other human in existence.

Collins has since said that he didn't feel any loneliness. 'Behind the Moon it was very peaceful – no one in mission control is yakkin' at me and wanting me to do this, that, and the other.' However, it's quite a long way to go to get some peace.

··················· **A SOLITARY FACT** ·····················

> In 2016, the remote Japanese train station of Kami-Shirataki was scheduled to close, until the authorities realised that a single student was still using it for her journey to school. They rescheduled the closure until after she graduated.

Can plants talk to each other and do they feel pain?

. . . .

Plants can communicate with each other, just not the way we do. They can send, receive and respond to signals without making a sound. They can physically feel things, and also have something similar to a sense of smell or taste.

Some plants communicate via fungi. Mushrooms are the visible part of a fungus, but underground there's a whole network of thin, white threads called mycelium. The mycelium link different plants together like an Internet super-highway or a telephone network. They transport water and nutrients, but also information in the form of chemical signals. In return, plants provide the fungi with food. The network can stretch from one end of a forest to the other.

Many forests have a 'mother tree' – a mature plant that acts as a hub. If young saplings aren't getting enough energy because the canopy is stopping light from getting through, they can signal that they need food, and the mother tree uses the mycelium network to pass sugar on to them.

The underground fungal network isn't confined to trees; if a tomato plant is attacked by an airborne fungus called blight, it can use the mycelium to warn others in the area. Broad beans can do this too: if one of them is attacked by aphids, it sends a signal to warn the surrounding broad bean plants that they should activate their anti-aphid defences. This system isn't always collaborative: some parasitic plants will use it to steal food from their hosts, while others use it to send out toxins to kill rivals.

Then there are plants that use the air to send a warning

signal when there is danger. The umbrella thorn acacia lives in sub-Saharan Africa, where giraffes sometimes eat its leaves. When they do, the tree sends out a chemical emergency signal, and other acacias pick up on the alarm. They start filling their leaves with a chemical called tannin, which makes them taste bitter, and the giraffes move on.

Grass can also send a warning. Many of us love the smell of freshly mown grass, but it's actually a distress signal. It is letting other patches of grass know that the lawnmower is coming, so that they can send precious sugars from their leaves down to their roots. If you start cutting the lawn at one end of your garden, the grass at the far end will 'smell' or 'hear' the alarm and will already be hunkering down before you get there with the mower.

Plants can communicate with insects too. If wild tobacco is being attacked by caterpillars, it can send out scents to attract other insects that will eat the caterpillars, or even attract parasitic wasps that will lay their eggs in the unsuspecting grub. If that particular tobacco plant doesn't survive, hopefully its neighbours will.

Plants cannot feel pain, because they don't have pain receptors, but they can sense when they are being damaged and can even distinguish between different types of attack. Beech and maple trees are able to tell if the damage is being caused by deer or by a human. When a deer bites a branch, the tree uses chemicals to make the leaves taste bad, but if a human breaks it, or if it's damaged by strong winds, the tree sends in substances to heal the wound. Plants such as snapdragons, orchids and peas know when they've been knocked over and will realign themselves into the correct position so they can be pollinated by insects.

Plants can even feel each other. Some trees can sense

when another tree gets too close, and so they leave a gap between them – it's called crown shyness. If you look up at the canopy in a forest, you can see spaces around each tree's set of branches, a bit like crazy paving. Nobody knows why they do this. Perhaps it is to allow more light in, or to prevent them injuring one another. Or maybe they just prefer their own space.

· · · · · · · · · · · · · · · · · · MUSHROOM FOR MORE? · · · · · · · · · · · · · · · · · ·

❯ The fungal network that plants communicate through is known as the wood wide web.

❯ Button, chestnut and portobello mushrooms are all the same species, harvested at different points in their growth cycle.

Can I put this in the recycling?

This book? Despite being made mostly of paper, probably not. Books are also full of binding glue, string and cloth, and often have a glossy dust jacket, all of which can be a problem for some recycling plants. You might have guessed that, because this book doesn't have a green arrows symbol on the back. But even if it did, things aren't always as they seem . . .

 The **interlocked arrows** do *not* mean that the packaging can be recycled, or even that it has ever been part of the recycling process. It means that the manufacturer has made a financial contribution to the recovery and recycling of packaging in Europe.

 The famous **three-arrowed triangle** means that the product is *theoretically* recyclable, although there is no guarantee that your local refuse-handling facility will be able to deal with it.

 A **white circular arrow in a green box** should give you the most confidence: it appears only on materials which are widely recycled by 75% or more of UK local authorities.

If you're seriously considering putting this book in the bin after reading it, please don't! At the very least, consider your downstairs loo.

How do plant seeds know which way is up?

After a seed is buried in soil, its first task is to work out where the surface is. Fortunately, seeds are perfectly designed to distinguish up from down. In fact, if you turn a seedling upside down halfway through sprouting, the stem will bend around to face upwards again within a few days.

Seed cells contain microscopic balls called statoliths. These act like pebbles in a jar, falling to the bottom of the cells thanks to the force of gravity. The seeds work out where the statoliths have come to rest and grow their roots downwards in that direction, while sending the stem the opposite way. You can channel your inner seed if you're ever trapped by an avalanche: make a pocket of air in front of your mouth, spit into it and see which way your saliva falls; that's the way gravity is working, so you should dig in the opposite direction.

THIS WAY DOWN!

A botanist called Thomas Knight was the first to show that seeds know which way is up. In 1805, he attached some to the outside of a wheel, which he then spun around 150 times a minute using water power from a stream in his garden. This caused centrifugal force to act on them – the same phenomenon that pins us against the back of a teacup ride when it spins in a fairground. The seeds, which couldn't tell the difference between this spinning force and the force of gravity, responded by growing their roots outwards and sending their stems inwards, until they met in the middle of the wheel.

❯ 32,000 years ago, an Ice Age squirrel buried some seeds in Siberia. In 2012, with the help of the Russian researchers who dug them up, they finally germinated and grew into white flowers.

Why do aeroplane window blinds have to be in the up position on take-off and landing?

Take-off and landing are the riskiest bits of a flight. In an emergency, the cabin crew's aim is to evacuate the whole plane in under 90 seconds. They open the blinds so that everyone's eyes can adjust to the natural light outside. Sudden changes in brightness are disorientating, but if your eyes have several minutes to adapt, you can see up to a thousand times better. This also applies when it's dark, which is why the crew dim the lights when taking off or landing at night.

Additionally, opening the blinds lets the cabin crew see out and the emergency services see in, meaning each can be aware of any dangers, such as blocked exits or fires.

At the end of the day, it's all done in the name of safety, so sit back, relax and enjoy your flight.

······················· **FACTWICK AIRPORT** ····················

❯ The world's first air stewardesses had a lot of extra duties, including screwing down loose seats, assisting with fuelling and pushing the plane into the hangar after the flight.

❯ In an effort to make planes lighter, faster and more efficient, Emirates are trialling virtual windows on their flights.

What is the deal with airline food?

The first problem is that any pie in the sky won't be very fresh. Safety regulations mean that the actual cooking is done on the ground, so a meal is cooked, frozen, packaged, stored for several hours, defrosted in the air and then reheated before it arrives at your tray table.

But even if you were presented with a perfectly prepared gourmet meal, you wouldn't be able to taste it in the same way that you would on the ground. The air pressure in an aeroplane's cabin is lower than at ground level (that's why your ears sometimes pop), and it can be very dry: the air is cleaned every few minutes, which removes a lot of the moisture. This affects how you taste things – or rather, how you smell things. The two senses are closely related, and up to 80% of the food you think you're tasting in your mouth you're actually smelling through the back of your nose, where nasal mucus captures odour molecules. But thin, dry aeroplane air evaporates this mucus, so it's less effective, meaning food smells and tastes bland.

A lot of thought goes into airline food, as eliminating even a few grams of weight can save airlines large amounts of money. In the 1980s, Robert Crandall, then head of American Airlines, calculated that if they removed just one olive from every salad served to passengers, nobody would notice, and the airline would save $40,000 a year. And in 2008, Northwest Airlines saved $500,000 by slicing limes into 16 pieces for its drinks service, instead of 10, meaning fewer were required for the drinks trolley.

Why do Canadian airport codes begin with a 'Y'?

The organisation in charge of the codes that are printed on your boarding passes and luggage tags is the International Air Transport Association (IATA). Some of these letters follow clear logic – like 'JFK' for New York's John F. Kennedy airport, or 'LHR' for London Heathrow – but IATA's master list is 8,965 airports long, and many of the codes appear to be much more random.

All 17 of Canada's international airports have codes that begin with a 'Y', and no one seems to know exactly why. The most persuasive theory we found is that it's because when three-letter airport codes were introduced, the Canadians adapted codes which they were already using to identify their cities' weather stations. The 'Y' signified that 'Yes', this was an airport with a weather station.

In an attempt to get to the bottom of this, we contacted IATA, who told us that using a 'Y' for Canada is not their rule and is something that has been requested by the airports themselves.

We wrote to Toronto airport and asked why they wanted the 'Y' in their code. They said that this is a question they get a lot, but they don't know the answer and usually point people to IATA, as they make the final decisions.

We decided against contacting IATA again, and didn't fancy emailing all 16 of Canada's other international airports for fear of being sucked into a never-ending feedback loop, but if you work for an airport, a weather station or can shed any more light on this, then please do email us at CanadianAirports@qi.com.

Why can planes fly through clouds but space rockets can't?

Lightning is extremely dangerous to aircraft, but it's also extremely common. On average, any aeroplane in commercial service around the world will get hit more than once a year. If you cancelled flights whenever there was a slight risk of an electrical storm, you'd be doing so every single day. To combat this, planes are fitted with protection, including an outer shell that has no gaps through which lightning can pass and fry the electronics.

You can't really do that with rockets, since many of their most important parts – such as the heat-resistant tiles – are on the outside. Also, they fly higher than commercial planes, where lightning is more frequent, and, worse still, their vapour trails can conduct electricity, making them a giant lightning rod. On top of all this, the dangerous nature of space means that even the smallest of mishaps can be fatal to the crew. Taking all that into consideration, take-offs are scheduled for when there is no lightning anywhere near the launch site.

It's not just the weather at the launch site that can cause problems. Space agencies have a number of sites around the world where rockets can land in an emergency. This means that a rocket launch in Florida can only go ahead if there is good weather in France, Spain and the Azores, among others. And, as the rocket might have to ditch in the sea, the space agency also needs to check that the waters between the US and Ireland are largely calm.

But even if there are multiple delays before take-off, the view from space will make it all worthwhile.

❯ In 1920, the *New York Times* published an editorial claiming that it was 'absurd' to believe that rockets would work in space. They issued a correction on 17 July 1969, the day after Apollo 11 launched.

❯ One of the first liquid-fuelled rockets was created as a publicity stunt for a 1920s German film about going to the Moon.

❯ The Russian space agency lights its rockets using giant wooden matchsticks.

How do you eat on the International Space Station?

．．．

The first meal in space was eaten by John Glenn in 1962. He had a sachet of apple sauce, a couple of sugar tablets and some water. The meals of today's space explorers are a far cry from that. The International Space Station (ISS)'s larder contains around a hundred different items, and before departure each astronaut can check in with the food scientists at Houston to sample 20–30 items that, if nutritious enough, can be added to the menu. A universal favourite is shrimp cocktail, which is added as a side dish to virtually every meal due to the fact that it has a much sharper flavour than any other space food. In 1995, astronaut Bill Gregory ate 48 meals in a row with shrimp cocktail on the side – including all his breakfasts.

Every few months an automated spacecraft loaded with fresh fruit, water and pre-packaged meals arrives at the ISS. If there's enough space in the medical sample freezer, ground control will occasionally send some ice cream as a treat.

Condiments like ketchup and mayonnaise are available on board, as are salt and pepper, but only as liquids as the little grains would get into machinery or the astronauts' eyes. For the same reason, normal bread would be an issue, so only tortillas are allowed as they don't leave any crumbs behind. The tortillas are extremely popular with astronauts but initially had to be specially made by NASA, as commercially available flatbreads had too short a shelf life. However, when Taco Bell released a new product that stayed fresh for nine months, NASA got out of the tortilla business.

So . . . how do astronauts go to the toilet in space?
The International Space Station has two toilets, but in truth they're little more than glorified vacuum pumps. To urinate, the astronauts are given a hose with a nozzle that has two attachments – one for men and one for women – to suck up the liquid. For defecation, there's a tiny hole that the astronauts have to squat over and aim into. There's a fan to keep the waste in place, and the astronauts themselves need to strap in to avoid floating away.

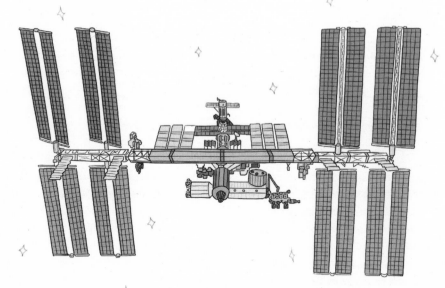

Occasionally, the toilet malfunctions and the waste floats around the cabin. Crews then have to catch it and return it to the toilet, a process that they have referred to as 'catching the brown trout'.

Once the toilet is full, an unlucky crew member has to don rubber gloves and pack down the solid waste. The water is removed and purified before being reused as drinking water or to rehydrate food, while the rest is stowed away, ready to be jettisoned into space, where it will eventually burn up in the Earth's atmosphere. This means that if you look up to the night sky and see a shooting star, there's a tiny chance that it might actually be the fiery demise of a brown trout.

························· **ORBITS AND PIECES** ·····················

❯ On astronaut Daniel Brandenstein's 47th birthday, he received an inflatable birthday cake as they couldn't get a real one up to him.

❯ In 2007, Swedish astronaut Christer Fuglesang wasn't allowed to have reindeer jerky on the ISS as the Americans were uncomfortable with it being eaten so close to Christmas. He replaced it with moose jerky.

❯ In 2002, ISS astronaut Peggy Whitson threatened to bar the entry of visiting astronauts from the space shuttle unless they brought her more hot sauce.

❯ In the 1980s, Pepsi spent $14,000,000 on developing a can that could be used in space. Astronauts didn't like it.

Which way would a helium balloon float in space?

A helium balloon is lighter than air, so on Earth it floats upwards, often resulting in an upset child. On the Moon, the air is much thinner, so the balloon would sink like a stone due to the Moon's gravity. Again, your child is probably going to be quite disappointed.

In the vast emptiness of space, there is no air – and no gravity – so in theory it would just stay where you left it. This sounds like good news for the child – except that the difference in pressure between the inside of the balloon and the vacuum of space means it would pop almost immediately.

Moral of the story: it's very difficult to keep children happy.

···················· UPLIFTING FACTS ····················

❯ The score for the choral work 'Song of the White Horse' instructs the singers to inhale helium before the high notes.

❯ When alligators inhale helium, their bellows sound deeper, not higher.

❯ A Canadian man inspired by the film *Up* tied over 100 helium balloons to his chair and got so high that commercial planes were flying beneath him. A judge described his actions as 'unconscionably stupid'.

Why don't clouds freeze?

They're usually already frozen.

Clouds are made of tiny droplets of water, which can be either liquid or (if it's cold enough) ice. But the ice crystals are so small and light that air currents from below stop them from falling out of the sky. As a cloud gets bigger, the ice starts sticking together, becoming heavier, and eventually heavy enough to start falling.

If the weather is cold enough, the ice crystals will stay frozen and become a snow shower; if it's warmer, they'll melt on the way down and become rain. So most of the rain that falls actually begins its life as snow.

················ **CIRRUS-LY GOOD FACTS** ··················

❯ The Cloud Appreciation Society has over 46,000 members in over 100 countries. Their manifesto begins: 'We believe that clouds are unjustly maligned and that life would be immeasurably poorer without them.'

❯ A group of bats is called a 'cloud'.

❯ HAT-P-7b, a planet over 1,000 light years away, has clouds made of rubies and sapphires.

How loud can something be?

. . . .

When the volcano Krakatoa erupted in 1883, it destroyed an island, threw debris 17 miles into the air, at a speed of half a mile a second, and killed 36,000 people. The noise it made was so loud that sailors 40 miles away suffered burst eardrums. Even 100 miles away, the volume was 170 decibels – loud enough to do lasting damage to those that heard it. And it could still be heard 3,000 miles away – the equivalent of a sound made in Britain being audible in the US. At its source, the sound was so loud that it went beyond what we mean by 'sound'.

All noises are the result of molecules knocking against each other, in a chain stretching from the source of the sound to your eardrum. When you snap your fingers, the air molecules surrounding them are disturbed. They then bump into their neighbours, and those molecules then pass that ripple of disturbance on to *their* nearest neighbours, and so on, until the sound hits your eardrum, which passes the message on to your brain. So while each molecule travels only a tiny distance, there's a *wave* of energy that makes it all the way from the source of the sound to your ear.

The wave consists of high-pressure areas with lots of molecules, followed by low-pressure areas that are relatively sparse. But once you get to a certain level (194 decibels, to be precise), there comes a point where the low-pressure regions are completely empty – there are no molecules in there at all. The sound can't get 'louder' than that, technically. If there is more energy in the noise source, the air molecules are just pushed along wholesale, rather than moving back and forth, and the soundwave has turned into a shockwave.

The shockwave from Krakatoa was so strong it circled the Earth four times.

. . . .

What is a decibel?
The decibel is named after Alexander Graham Bell, but a single 'bel' is so large that scientists tend to divide it by 10, giving us a 'decibel'.

. . . .

Decibel levels
The sound of your own breathing	10 dB
A whisper	20 dB
A normal conversation	60 dB
A noisy restaurant	70 dB
An electric drill	95 dB
Jill Drake, a teaching assistant who recorded the loudest shout ever in 2000	129 dB

Where does the phrase 'stealing someone's thunder' come from?

In 1709, playwright John Dennis staged a production of *Appius and Virginia*, a tragedy set in ancient Rome. Critics didn't like the show but were impressed by a new 'thunder machine' that had been built to create sound effects for stormy scenes.

Appius and Virginia ran for only a few nights and was soon replaced by a production of *Macbeth*. When Dennis turned up to watch the Scottish Play, he was shocked to hear his distinctive sound effect being used: they had literally stolen his thunder.

········· **EN-LIGHTNING FACTS** ·········

❯ The word 'astonishing' comes from the Latin *tonare*, meaning 'thunder'.

❯ The only man to have been struck by lightning seven times and survived is ex-park ranger Roy C. Sullivan. The seventh time he was struck coincided with the 22nd time he had fought off a bear with a stick.

❯ Engineers have developed a weapon called the 'electrolaser' that can shoot lightning bolts.

Why is a group of crows called a 'murder'?

The Book of Saint Albans, by Dame Juliana Berners, was a guide for 15th-century gentlemen on how to behave in polite society without embarrassing themselves. It was remarkable for a few reasons: it was the first English book with a section on fishing, the first to use colour printing and one of the first to be written by a woman. It also gave us some colourful names for groups of animals, including a 'business' of ferrets, a 'gaggle' of geese and a 'murder' of crows – terminology that we still use today.

Berners probably didn't come up with these herself; she was just writing down terms that were in common use and which reflected the experiences of medieval hunters. Geese make a gaggling noise; ferrets often seem busy ('busyness' and 'business' used to mean the same thing); and a group of crows was probably called a 'murder' due to their grizzly reputation and links to the occult – they were thought to be omens of death or possibly witches in disguise, and could often be seen pecking at corpses on bloody battlefields.

While some of these collective nouns date back hundreds of years, many of the more fun ones are relatively modern. We have no evidence of anyone referring to a 'bloat' of hippopotamuses before a fishing manual of 1939; a 'parliament' of owls was invented by C. S. Lewis in his *Narnia* series; and our favourite, a 'blessing' of unicorns, is only around 20 years old – before that they were a plain old 'herd'.

Do cats get goosebumps?

They do. When animals such as cats, dogs and chimpanzees get goosebumps, it causes their hairs to stand on end, making them appear bigger and fluffier. This is useful for a couple of reasons. One is that the straighter hairs trap a layer of insulating air against the skin, which helps them to stay warm when it's cold. Another is that it makes them appear larger to potential predators or rivals, which could scare them off. Goosebumps haven't been much use to us ever since we lost most of our body hair. We still experience them, though, whenever we get cold or frightened.

Can animals give blood?

The first recipients of blood transfusions were animals. In 1666, the year of the Great Fire of London, scientists used the feather of a goose as a tube to move blood from one dog to another. They had worked out that blood was important for life, but didn't know exactly what it did. Some scientists thought that taking the blood of a hungry dog would make the recipient hungry; or that if you taught one dog how to fetch a stick, you could transfer that knowledge through a transfusion.

Sadly, that first dog died during the operation, and it would be 150 years before the technique was safe enough to be tried successfully on humans, but today blood transfusions in dogs are relatively routine procedures. The Royal Veterinary College in London administers around 600 transfusions to pets every year. There are even pet blood banks that your dog or cat can donate to, but they must be healthy, up to date on their vaccinations and 'easy to handle'.

For non-mammals, it's a bit more complicated. Different species of fish have different types of blood, so you can't give trout blood to a goldfish, for instance. Bird blood is interchangeable, so theoretically a robin could donate blood to an ostrich, though you would need rather a lot of them.

Who is faster, Usain Bolt or a fly?

Usain Bolt is the fastest human ever. He could run 100 metres in just 9.58 seconds, with a top speed of almost 28 mph, which is comfortably above the 20 mph speed limit in force outside schools in the UK.

If Bolt raced against a fly, his success would depend upon the species of his opponent, as top speeds vary between flies. A housefly goes at only around 4 mph, so the race would literally be a walk in the park for Usain. Horseflies, on the other hand, are much faster. When a male is chasing after a female, they can reach 90 mph. Bolt has nothing on that.

One candidate for an even faster insect is the deer botfly. In 1926, an American scientist called Charles Townsend claimed that he had seen one of them travelling at 400 yards per second (that's more than 800 mph, faster than the fastest passenger plane today). His story made the pages of the *New York Times*. If this measurement was accurate, a deer botfly would be able to complete a 100-metre race in about the same time as it would take Bolt to react to the sound of the starter pistol. However, we now think that Townsend's measurements were flawed: any insect flying that fast would have to eat more than its own body weight in food to keep up the speed, and the G force would be enough to crush its head.

Bolt may be the fastest human, but in the animal kingdom it's not just horseflies that leave him in their dust: cheetahs, neon flying squids and even domestic cats can run faster than him. However, his trainer has said he's never run for a full mile non-stop, so if you can do that, then you've run further than the fastest man on the planet – if not at the same speed.

Why is it almost impossible to swat a fly?

Flies are masters of not being swatted. A fruit fly, for example, has two eyes like us, but each one is made up of around 800 smaller visual receptors called ommatidia, which relay information to the fly's brain. They're pointing in all different directions, meaning that a fly sees a world made of lots of tiny images and can detect movement in an almost 360° field of view.

By filming flies with high-speed cameras, we know they can react to the threat of the swat within a tenth of a second. In that time, their brain, which is the size of a poppy seed, has worked out an escape plan, placed the fly's legs in the best position to dart out of the way and launched it into flight.

We can't beat a fly through speed, but we just might with a bit of cunning. A good tactic is not to swat at its starting point, but to try and anticipate where it might jump to next. Or you could just let it buzz around in peace.

· FAST FACTS ·

❯ In the next edition of the *OED*, the word with the most definitions is expected to be 'run', which has 645 meanings in the verb form alone.

❯ Despite their pudgy appearance, wombats have a top speed of 25 mph – almost as fast as Usain Bolt.

Who would win in a swimming race, a human, a fish or a mermaid?

The most decorated Olympian of all time, swimmer Michael Phelps, is also known as 'The Superfish' or 'The Flying Fish'. He has won 28 medals, which means that if he were a country, he would rank higher than Portugal and Nigeria on the Olympic leaderboard and be only three medals behind Ireland.

In 2017, as part of 'Shark Week', the Discovery Channel decided to test whether Phelps could outswim a shark. To make things a bit fairer, Phelps was given a fin to help him to glide through the water; and to make things a bit safer, the shark was digitally created. In the end, the shark won, completing the 100m race in 36.1 seconds, two seconds ahead of Phelps. Phelps's response: 'Rematch? Next time, warmer water.'

So fish can beat humans, especially in cold water, but could a mermaid give you the best of both worlds? A straight-up race is unlikely, but Katherine Davies and Faeeza Lorgat at the University of Leicester have done the maths. They looked at a half-human/half-dolphin hybrid and concluded that the upper-body strength of the human plus the tail strength of the dolphin would be an unbeatable combination. However, their comparison holds true only if the mermaid can hold her breath, if her skin creates similar drag to a dolphin's and, crucially, if she actually exists.

Why do some fish have scales but others don't?

A fish's scales are for protection. They're made from very thin bone which grows out of their skin and acts like a suit of armour. Despite being covered in tiny bony plates, scaly fish are still flexible because their scales overlap and pass over each other as they bend.

Fish without scales use different strategies to stay safe. Scaleless eels, for example, are covered in a thick layer of slimy mucus that protects their skin, while pufferfish can swallow enough water to make themselves large and spherical, which makes it harder for predators to eat them.

The scales on a fish can also tell you how old it is. Every year, the fish will have a summer growth spurt, when there is plentiful food, followed by a period of slower growth, a process that results in a visible ring. You can count these rings as you would the rings on a tree to get the age of the fish in years. It's not foolproof, but it gives a decent estimation, which is useful to scale experts – or squamatologists, as they're more formally known.

Why aren't monorails more popular?

The future overtook them.

There are two types of monorail. In one the carriages sit astride the rail; in the other they hang below it. And they're much older than you might think. The first one was up and running three months before the first passenger steam train. It was of the hanging-down type and ran for three-quarters of a mile in Hertfordshire. It was built to transport bricks from a brickworks down to the river for shipping, but they added a novelty open-topped carriage at the front so that sightseers could go along just for fun. The 'engine' was a single horse.

The Greater London Council once looked into using monorails but decided that they wouldn't improve things. Monorails tend to be slow, expensive and a blot on the landscape. Because they run on a single track, trains have to be wrapped around it so they don't fall off, meaning it's much more complicated (and more costly) to make points that would switch them to another track. A whole section of the concrete support would have to move, rather than just the rails, as with a normal train.

Monorails featured in a *Simpsons* episode called 'Marge vs the Monorail', in which a con man convinces the town of Springfield to install a 'bona fide, electrified' monorail system, and it ends in disaster. The Monorail Society said this was unfair to monorails, which it claims are safe, green and good value for money. But the editor of *Railnews* told the BBC: 'Monorails seem like a good idea until you actually use them.'

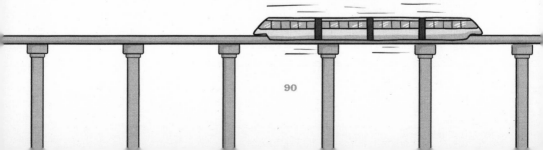

What is the origin of the phrase 'back to square one'?

The most common explanation is that before football was on television every day, if you wanted to experience the thrill of the game, you had to either go to the match or listen to it on the radio. And it wasn't always easy for listeners to work out what was going on, since the action moved so quickly. To make things simpler, in the late 1920s magazines began to publish a plan of the pitch overlaid with numbered squares. When the ball was near the goal, the commentator would say the action was in square seven or eight, and when it was passed back to the defenders, it might go 'back to square one'.

However, we don't think this is the case. Firstly, that's not really how football was played in the 1920s. There was a lot less patient passing between the defenders and a lot more lumping the ball forward as quickly as possible. Also, the pitch plans were phased out by the 1930s, and the idiom wasn't seen in print until the 1950s. The first example we have of anyone using the phrase comes in a review of a particularly complicated book about American economics, where the reader is 'always being sent back to square one in a sort of intellectual game of snakes and ladders'. And that's a clue to the actual origin. We think it's simply referring to games such as snakes and ladders or hopscotch, in which players might incur a penalty and be sent back to the start.

Was there a real person called Gordon Bennett?

Gordon Bennett – full name James Gordon Bennett Jr – was born in 1841, the same year as King Edward VII. He was a wealthy bachelor, and the tales of his misbehaviour were legendary. He drove his carriage through New York naked, rode his horse into a gentlemen's club, would pull the covers off restaurant tables just to hear the crockery smash, and once threw a roll of banknotes into a fire because he didn't like the way they felt in his pocket. He turned up to his own engagement party so drunk that he mistook his future father-in-law's fireplace for a urinal and relieved himself in full view of the other guests. It's not entirely fair to relate that story as absolute fact: some sources say he urinated into a grand piano. Either way, the marriage did not go ahead.

He eventually married for the first time at 73, but died just four years later. His plan for his own memorial was typically outlandish. He wanted a 200ft pillar, with a sarcophagus in the shape of an owl, to tower over New York from the highest point of Manhattan. The top of the owl was to be 150ft higher than the Statue of Liberty's crown, and Bennett wanted it to be hollow so that visitors could look through the owl's eyes and take in the sights of the city. Sadly, it was never built, but Bennett's excess in life meant that his name lives on whenever anyone exclaims GORDON BENNETT!

Why are men's buttons on the right and women's on the left?

It's a consequence of how rich people used to get dressed.

Affluent women used to have a lady's maid to help them get ready, and placing the buttons on the left makes it easier for a right-handed person who is facing you to use their dominant hand to guide each button in. Men of the same status would have dressed themselves, and so the theory applies in reverse. Fashion was, for centuries, dictated by the upper classes, and it's likely this style began there and filtered down through society, remaining in place today.

But not everyone loves buttons: Steve Jobs famously suffered from koumpounophobia (the fear of buttons), and it's been argued that that's the reason we have touch-screen phones today.

················ **FASCINATING FASTENINGS** ················

❭ Over 60% of all buttons are made in Qiaotou, China, which is also known as 'Button City'.

❭ Einstein invented a blouse with two sets of buttons, so the owner could still wear it if they put on weight.

When we say 'happy as Larry', who is Larry?

If you look this up online, you'll keep coming across Larry Foley, a late-19th-century Irish–Australian boxer. He was part of a Catholic street-fighting gang that was embroiled in a turf war with local Protestants. He had a reputation as a hard man, and one day the Protestants' best fighter, Sandy Ross, called him out. Ross was bald, with a broad head that he used with great effect to butt his opponents. But Foley was nimble, and the fight went on for 71 rounds before the police stepped in and put a stop to it.

Foley later turned professional. The story goes that when he won his final fight, he received a huge payout. The resulting headlines read 'Happy as Larry', and so the phrase was born. Sadly, though it's true that 'happy as Larry' was definitely first said Down Under, it's also true people were saying it in 1875 – four years before Foley quit.

So, the question of who Larry was, and why he was so happy, is still up for grabs.

One theory is that Larry was a popular name among Irish migrants to Australia in the 1800s, who were often said to have a 'happy-go-lucky' attitude. Another suggestion is that 'Larry' is short for the Aussie word *larrikin*, meaning a 'scoundrel' or 'rogue', or it could come from *larrie*, an old Scottish word meaning 'joke'.

Larry Foley was a real person, though. He introduced the Queensberry Rules to Australia and is known as the 'Father of Australian Boxing'. Generous and popular, he died in 1917, after collapsing in a Turkish bath. A huge crowd came to his funeral, including all of his seven children and the mayor of Sydney.

As the ancient Greek philosopher Solon said, 'Call no man happy until he is dead.'

. . . .

Who were the sandboys in the phrase 'happy as a sandboy'?

Before sawdust came along, 'sandboys' were men (or boys) who were paid to fetch sand from beaches to spread on the floor of pubs and theatres to soak up spills. They weren't especially happy at work – but they cheered up immensely after a few beers.

. . . .

Who were Tom, Dick and Harry?

When the phrase first emerged in the 1600s, these were just three common names. In 1835, Charles Darwin brought three giant tortoises home on *The Beagle*, which he called Tom, Dick and Harry. But 'Harry' turned out to be female, so was quickly renamed Harriet.

When did it become fashionable for a smartly dressed man to wear a tie or bow tie?

The first cravats were found on the battlefield. The Thirty Years' War began in 1618 and was a conflict between western Europe's Catholics and Protestants. While both opponents felt they had God on their side, there was one faction that was just happy to fight for the highest bidder: the Croatian *crabats*, a group of mercenaries who were known for their horsemanship, cruelty and sartorial elegance. They wore tall fur hats, long red cloaks and, crucially, cloth around their necks to keep their jackets tight.

When peace returned, civilians took to wearing similar loose-fitting cloths, calling them 'cravats', after the Croatian soldiers. The young French King Louis XIV was a fan and decided it would become de rigueur in his court for people to wear a necktie. Where Louis's court led, fashion followed – not just in Paris, but throughout Europe and into the Americas.

The new fashion had its variations. While the aristocrats of Paris wore cravats made of expensive lace, American workers were able to use cheaper cloth. And the size varied too, including one cravat that covered the bottom of the face in its entirety. Eventually, thanks to its neatness and the convenience of it not flailing in the breeze, a bow tie became the neckwear of choice for the well-dressed gentleman. Abraham Lincoln wore one, as did Winston Churchill. However, after the Second World War its popularity declined and it became virtually unknown outside of formal wear, but no one is quite sure why. In 1996, the Neckwear Association of America revealed that only 3% of the 100 million ties sold each year in the US were bow ties. And in 2014, a survey of 8,900 American men revealed that only 1% knew how to tie one.

Despite this decline, the bow tie still has an occasional resurgence in popularity. When Matt Smith joined the cast of *Doctor Who* in 2010, proudly wearing a bow tie, sales in the UK doubled within a month. And it's not just fictional doctors who like them. As one paediatrician working at the Children's Hospital of Philadelphia said: 'It's much more difficult for a baby to pee on your tie if it's a bow tie.'

. . . .

When did chefs start to wear big white hats?
This is also a fashion that spread from France. The great 18th-century Parisian chef Marie-Antoine Carême thought the floppy hats worn by his cooks made them look as if they were wearing a nightcap and ready for bed, so he added cardboard to make the hats tall and stiff, which he thought gave the chefs more authority. More experienced staff received taller hats, and he gave himself one that was 18 inches in height – about the length of a house cat.

Dogs are man's best friend, but do other animals have friends?

Interspecies relationships are very rare, except in a domestic setting (think of a cat and a dog snuggled together), but some animals do form social bonds – what we call friendship – with other members of the same species.

Chimpanzees, like people, choose chimpanzee friends that have similar personalities to their own. Extroverts spend time with extroverts, and shy chimps hang out with other shy chimps. They trust their friends more than they trust strangers.

Vampire bats form friendships that can last for decades. They begin by grooming each other, and later, once they trust each other, they will share a meal, with one regurgitating blood to feed the other.

Some animals that live in groups spend more time with the same small clique than they do with other members of the group, just like we do. We're not necessarily friends with everyone at work or in our classroom. Cows live in herds but have another cow that they like to eat hay with, and they become stressed if they are separated. Garter snakes form a gang with a few others to whom they stay physically close. Flamingos have best friends that they keep for years and with whom they spend all their time in the flock, but they also seem to have enemies, or at least some birds that they don't get on with and avoid.

An important aspect of friendship is empathy. We will comfort a companion when they are distressed; we understand how they feel and try to do something about it. Elephants also show empathy, caressing an upset elephant with their trunk while making small chirruping noises, while ravens console their friends if they've been attacked by another bird.

So although we can't know exactly how animals are feeling, we can identify behaviour that suggests friendship is not solely a human trait.

· ·

Who coined the phrase 'man's best friend'?
The first person to name a dog as his 'best friend' was Frederick the Great of Prussia (1712–86). He wanted to be buried next to his beloved greyhounds, but instead was laid to rest next to his father, whom he hated. His body was eventually moved and placed beside his pets in 1991.

· **FRIENDLY FACTS** ·

❯ Crows not only hold grudges, they tell their friends and family about them.

❯ A tiger in a Siberian zoo made friends with a goat that had been put in his enclosure as a meal.

❯ Google's company policy states that they prefer dogs to cats.

❯ Sled dogs have been working with humans for at least 9,500 years.

Why don't cats and dogs have belly buttons?

Almost all mammals have a belly button – the scar that remains once the umbilical cord is cut – but there are a couple of exceptions. Marsupials, such as kangaroos and koalas, don't have them because they develop in pouches and are so young when they lose their cords that it doesn't leave a mark. There are also some mammals that hatch from eggs, like the duck-billed platypus and the echidna; they never grow an umbilical cord in the first place.

Cats and dogs do have them; they just don't look like human ones. When they are born, the puppy's or kitten's mother bites off the umbilical cord, leaving a small, flat scar on their stomach. This is their equivalent of a belly button. Fur soon grows over it, making it trickier to observe, but if you see a dog or cat rolling on their back, you may be able to spot it.

This small belly button is typical of mammals; it's actually humans who have unusually big ones. Because it takes a lot of nutrients to nourish a human foetus, we have a relatively large umbilical cord for our size. When it is cut, instead of leaving a tiny mark it leaves a hole (or a bump if you're one of the 10% of people with an 'outie'), which is unique in the animal kingdom.

· · · · · · · · · · · · · · · · · · **A NAVEL-GAZING FACT** · · · · · · · · · · · · · · · · · · ·

❯ Barbie didn't have a belly button until she turned 40 years old.

Why is 'squirrel-proof' bird food covered in chilli?

A chilli plant wants its seeds to be eaten and spread, because that's how they reproduce. Some creatures are better at this job than others. Birds are the best distributors because they cover large distances and don't digest the seeds, excreting them whole. Mammals, on the other hand, grind up the seeds with their teeth and damage them with their digestive juices. By the time a seed has been eaten by a squirrel and emerged out of the other end, it's often completely destroyed.

To deter these predators, chillies evolved to produce capsaicin, the chemical that gives them their hot, spicy flavour. Most mammals hate this heat, but birds can't feel it. That's why they will happily gobble up chilli seeds and chilli-coated bird food, while other animals, like squirrels, stay away.

So why do humans like chilli?
We're suckers for punishment. When we eat chilli, it stimulates pain receptors, and our brain responds with natural pain relief in the form of endorphins and dopamine. These chemicals give us a high, so we keep going back for more.

····················· **A RED-HOT FACT** ·····················

❯ Nando's have said that they often get men on dates who ask for plain chicken with an 'Extra Hot' flag in it.

Do ducks actually like bread?

Ducks love eating bread, but *too much* of it is a problem because it fills them up and stops them from consuming more nutritious food. Essentially, bread is junk food for ducks. Birds that eat a lot of white bread are at risk of both malnutrition and becoming so obese that they are unable to fly or escape from predators.

To combat this, advice was issued in 2015 saying that people shouldn't feed bread to ducks, but they could instead offer sweetcorn, peas, oats or worms. Unfortunately, this backfired because most people just stopped feeding them altogether. This led to ducks going hungry, so some parks now have signs up asking the public to please start feeding bread to their ducks again. Like all junk food, it's fine in moderation.

· · · · · · · · · · · · · · · · · · · QUICK QUACK FACTS · · · · · · · · · · · · · · · · · · ·

❯ Foods you must never feed to ducks include chocolate, potatoes, onions, beans and avocados.

❯ A group of ducks on water is called a paddling.

❯ Bangladeshi farmers are raising ducks instead of chickens because when floods come, the birds can survive by floating.

If I take a swan to the vet, does the Queen have to pay?

For hundreds of years, swans in England were branded by their owners by etching symbols into their beaks. The Crown did this as well but, just to be safe, it made a rule that any unmarked mute swan belonged to the monarchy. However, HM the Queen only exercises control over swans around Windsor and certain stretches of the Thames (between Sunbury and Abingdon), a fact that five-year-old Lyndsay Simpson found out when she asked Her Majesty for a pet swan in 2017.

Since the 13th century, there has been an annual counting of the swans on the Thames, undertaken by the Royal Swan Markers, who spend the third week of July rowing up the river in their fancy red jackets, counting swans and cygnets and giving them little ankle bracelets to make sure they're all accounted for.

The Crown also owns all whales, sturgeon and porpoises if they are caught near the English coast or find themselves washed up on an English beach. Don't try to sell one, though, because even if Buckingham Palace doesn't want it, these animals are endangered enough to be protected by international law.

So if you took the right swan to the vet, technically the Queen would be liable to pay, but in practice you'd probably be left with the bill. Along with the rest of the swan.

Are Nice biscuits pronounced 'nice' or 'niece'?

It used to be 'nice' due to their nice taste, but when Queen Victoria visited the French Riviera in 1882 and took the biscuits with her, the pronunciation was officially changed to 'niece' (like the French city of Nice, which rhymes with 'geese'). However, even after almost 150 years, 80% of people still pronounce the name the old way.

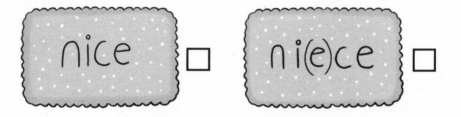

················· FRESHLY BAKED FACTS ·················

> In New Zealand's parliament, members' bills that may be debated in future are stored in a 30-year-old biscuit tin known as 'the biscuit tin of democracy'.

> As a special treat, the ravens in the Tower of London are fed biscuits soaked in blood.

> French digestive biscuits come with the slogan 'It's English, but it's good!'

When did salted caramel become so popular?

About the same time as Chewbacca.

Salted caramels were invented in 1977 – the year *Star Wars* was released. They were the work of French chocolatier Henri Le Roux, who was inspired by the salted butter of Brittany. They were an instant hit. In the first year of sales, the 48,000 Caramels au Beurre Salé sold weighed almost as much as a grand piano; nearly double that quantity were bought in year two; and in 1980, they won the coveted title of 'Best Sweet in France'.

In the 1990s, Parisian pastry chef Pierre Hermé created a salted caramel macaron, which sparked a craze among New York foodies and began the flavour's rise to worldwide fame. Soon, top restaurants were adding salt to their desserts. Then, in 2008, things really took off: Häagen-Dazs launched salted caramel ice cream, Starbucks introduced salted caramel hot chocolate, and Barack Obama revealed that his favourite sweets were sea-salt chocolate caramels from a shop in Seattle. At the peak of its popularity, you could buy salted caramel green tea, salted caramel Pepsi and even salted caramel-flavoured Pringles.

Americans have always had a fondness for sweet-and-salty combinations, from Snickers bars to Hawaiian pizza. As US food writer Dorie Greenspan said of salted caramel: 'The combination is so natural for Americans we should be annoyed at ourselves that we didn't invent it.'

What's the difference between a macaroon and a macaron?

A macaroon is made with coconuts; a macaron with almonds. But they used to be the same thing.

The confusion between macaroons and macarons begins in the 9th century, when Muslim troops invaded Sicily from North Africa. Though Arab rule would be relatively short-lived, its influence on the local culture was enormous and permanent, especially in the kitchen. The Arabs brought rice (used in risotto), the aubergine (the star of Sicily's signature dish *pasta alla Norma*), and they also brought nut-based sweets.

Before the invasion, Sicilian cuisine centred round pasta. You might have savoury cheesy pasta for your main course and a sweet pasta for dessert. It didn't take long for Italian pudding recipes to combine with the Arab taste for confectionery, and the nutty biscuits first known as *maccarruni* were born.

When the almond biscuits reached France, they acquired a more Gallic-sounding name, macarons. When they got to Britain, they became macaroons. (French words often gained an extra 'o' crossing the Channel – 'balloon', 'cartoon' and 'saloon', for example.) But, despite their different names, macarons and macaroons were still basically the same: both were made from almonds, sugar and egg whites.

The Americans got involved when the US was gripped by a sudden craze for coconuts in the 19th century. The macaroon was given a makeover and the traditional almond paste was replaced by shredded coconut.

Around the same time, the French came up with another innovation. Macarons were often sold in pairs, so a Parisian baker had the idea of sandwiching them together with a *ganache*, or almond paste, filling. These evolved into the colourful treats that decorate Instagram today.

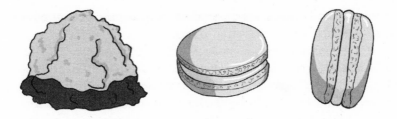

Now we have two distinct types: the dainty Parisian macaron and the chewier Anglo-Saxon macaroon. Double the biscuit means double the fun. So, if you're looking for an excuse to enjoy them, National Macaron Day is celebrated on 20 March, while National Macaroon Day is on 31 March.

. . . .

Why are petits fours given that name?
In French, the word *four* means 'oven'. Bakers' ovens were traditionally very large and heated to a high temperature. When they were turned off each day, the ovens would take a while to cool down, and in order not to waste that heat, bakers learned to make delicate pastries in the cooler temperatures. The petit four comes from this innovation: the 'small oven' was actually a cooler, less powerful one.

HR SGHR Z BNCD?

You might assume this question is in code, but actually it's a cipher. There's a difference.

A code is when whole words or phrases are converted into strings of nonsensical characters – or even different, misleading words. For example, if you received the coded message **SWEEP THE PATIO** and had the correct decoding book, you would look up the word **SWEEP** and find that it means **INVADE**, and then look up **PATIO** and find that it means **TOWN**. So the decoded message is **INVADE THE TOWN**.

The drawback is that you have to assign a code to every phrase you want to send, so code books would be quite big, like a dictionary. But messages can be shortened with code, saving time and space: the code **BLUE! PANDA!** could mean **THE ENEMY IS INVADING! SEND REINFORCEMENTS!**

Ciphers, on the other hand, simply take every individual character and substitute it for another one, using a set of rules. The question at the top of the page was encrypted by shifting every letter back one place in the alphabet. So, to decrypt it, you need to shift the letters forward again. 'A' becomes 'B', 'B' becomes 'C', etc., so it reads: **IS THIS A CODE?**

If you don't have codes or ciphers to hand, you may have to resort to other methods to keep your correspondence secret. According to ancient historian Herodotus, Histiaeus, the leader of the Persians, once sent a message by shaving a slave's head and tattooing the words onto his scalp. After his hair had grown back, the slave was sent to Aristagoras, the leader of the city of Miletus, who then shaved the man's head again to reveal the memo, which informed him that the Persian army was about to invade – presumably marching there extremely slowly.

Duvets have 'tog ratings', but what is a tog?

The tog is a way of measuring how well something stops heat from escaping. It was developed during the Second World War by the Shirley Institute, a research centre for cotton technologies, to help manufacturers to create better clothing for British troops. Today it's almost only ever used to measure how warm duvets are.

There were no duvets in Britain during wartime; in fact, they didn't come over from the Continent until the 1950s, when they were known as 'continental quilts'. They were greeted with suspicion as a strange foreign habit, until the sheer convenience converted people. In the 1960s, the shop Habitat advertised that duvets meant you could make your bed in 10 seconds, rather than doing lots of complicated tucking-in. Some institutions held out for much longer: Windsor Castle only switched from sheets and blankets to duvets in 2016.

The word 'tog' dates back to 1708, and it was an abbreviation of 'togman', a kind of cloak or loose coat. Ultimately, it derives from the Latin item of clothing the toga – which, rather pleasingly, is an item of clothing that looks like a bedsheet.

BEDUCATION

❯ The record for fastest bed-making is 69 seconds.

❯ Some hotels provide a pillow menu.

❯ In Australia, bed linen is often called 'Manchester', due to the English city's close association with the cotton industry.

Why is the weekend only two days long?

In 19th-century Britain, lots of people worked from Tuesday to Saturday, then had Sunday off – when they frequently drank and partied. They often ended up so hungover that they would bunk off on Monday and refuse to go into work, claiming they were observing 'Saint Monday' – a kind of joke saint's day. 'Saint Monday' was unofficial and bosses hated it; not only was it the result of drunkenness, but it was also the day for violent, uncivilised sports like cockfighting.

In response, workers' unions and religious bodies argued it might be better to lengthen the official weekend. Factory bosses were urged to give people half of Saturday off, in the hope it would make them more efficient and get rid of the Monday hangovers. Saturday afternoon was marketed as a time when workers could enjoy 'rational recreation', like gardening or going to museums.

Anti-alcohol campaigners joined the campaign for a day-and-a-half break lasting from Saturday lunchtime till Monday morning, hoping it might help workers to battle the demon drink. Then, in the 1880s, football matches started being played on Saturday, which drew in more people to this new nearly-weekend.

The first company to install a proper two-day weekend on Saturday and Sunday was a mill in New England in 1908, which made Saturday an official day off out of respect for the Jewish Sabbath. In 1926, Henry Ford started giving all his factory workers a full weekend off too – he reasoned that the more free time people had, the more cars he might sell.

In the UK, the first weekend came in 1934, courtesy of Boots, when its chairman, John Boot, experimented with giving his workers extra time off instead of making redundancies. The idea caught on, and 'Saint Monday' has hardly been heard of since.

· ·

Why is October not the eighth month, seeing as 'oct' means 'eight'?

In ancient Rome, there were only ten months, and the eighth was October. The last 60 or so days of the year, when no crops would grow, were not assigned to any month. The system had obvious flaws, so a king called Numa Pompilius inserted two new months at the top of the year: January, named after Janus, the two-headed god who could look both back into the past and forward into the future; and February, named after Februa, an end-of-winter celebration.

· · · · · · · · · · · · · · SOMETHING FOR THE WEEKEND · · · · · · · · · · · · · · ·

❭ Up to 33% of the British workforce does some work at weekends.

❭ There have been other weekend experiments in history. Ancient Romans had a day off every eight days, the French Revolution gave people one day off in 10, and the Soviet Union tried having no weekends from 1929 to 1940, instead giving people random days off during their working week, before scrapping the idea.

❭ In 1965, the US Senate predicted that in the year 2000, people would be working a 14-hour week.

Why do we get instant coffee but not instant tea?

Instant coffee is made by brewing the drink as normal, then dehydrating it to form crystals. When you add water, the crystals dissolve, and the flavour is infused into the water. In theory, there's no reason why you can't do something similar with tea, and in fact instant tea was drunk in China for over a thousand years.

The Chinese instant tea was called *cha gao*. It was made by boiling tea for two to three days, until it became little more than a dark sludge at the bottom of the pot. The sludge dried into a black lump that turned into tea when you added water. It was considered so delicious and delicate that it became the tea of choice for the elite, and poorer people weren't allowed to drink it. When the ruling Qing dynasty fell in 1911, it marked the end of China's imperial era, and the end of the golden age of instant tea.

Other, more industrial techniques for instant tea have been invented, but they've never really caught on because tea bags are just so convenient. In fact, their very invention came as a result of looking to save time. When tea bags were first created at the turn of the 20th century, customers were supposed to remove the tea leaves from the bags and use the product in loose-leaf form. However, tea-drinkers quickly realised it was much easier to leave the tea in the porous bags, and so the tea bag that we have come to know and love was born.

Is it true that drinking a cup of tea on a hot day will cool you down?

If you drink something hot, your body is tricked into thinking you're too warm, so it does what it always does when you overheat and sweats. Researchers confirmed this by instructing (presumably quite fit) study participants to ride an exercise bike for 75 minutes while drinking water of varying temperatures. The hotter the water, the more sweat they produced. As sweat evaporates from your skin, it takes away a portion of your body heat with it and cools you down.

In another experiment, scientists pumped hot water directly into people's stomachs through a tube and compared their sweat levels with those of people who only rinsed their mouths with it. The first group produced much more sweat, thereby proving that the deception occurs when the hot tea hits the stomach, and that gargling with tea and spitting it out is not an effective way to cool down.

EXTRA SHOTS

❯ In the tea industry, the term 'tea leaves' is saved for full leaves from the tea plant. The small leaf particles in tea bags are not tea leaves but 'fannings'.

❯ During the American Civil War, a common coffee substitute was ground acorns.

❯ Four cups of decaffeinated coffee can contain as much caffeine as one regular coffee.

❯ Saliva strips away 300 of the 631 chemicals that make up the aroma of coffee, which is why it seems to taste worse than it smells.

Should the tea or the milk go in first?

It depends on who you ask. The British Standards Institute (BSI) has a 10-page report on the right way to make a cup of tea, and it says you should put the *milk* in first. Chemical engineer Dr Andrew Stapley agrees. His 2002 study found that adding cold milk to hot tea can heat the milk unevenly and spoil the taste.

But that is by no means everyone's view. In George Orwell's 1946 essay 'A Nice Cup of Tea', he argued for *tea* first, so that you can add just the right amount of milk. The makers of Yorkshire Tea, Tetley and PG Tips all think so too. If you're making tea in a mug rather than a teapot, they say you should pour the hot water onto the teabag first, as putting the milk in first gets in the way of a proper brew.

Tea and milk weren't always an obvious pairing. In China, people have been drinking tea on its own for 5,000 years, and even now the BSI provides guidelines for tea with or without milk. Tea didn't reach Britain until the 1600s, and was initially taken as a medicine, before it was popularised as a drink by Catherine of Braganza, the Portuguese wife of King Charles II. In those days, it was only for the rich, and was so expensive that it was often kept under lock and key. The first person to suggest adding milk was an English tea merchant called Thomas Garway. In around 1670, he put out an advertisement listing all the health benefits of drinking tea. Adding milk, he said, helped to avoid loose bowels.

Tea went on to become the essence of Britishness. So much so that when King George VI became the first reigning

monarch to visit the US in 1939, President Roosevelt took the trouble to provide the royal party with 'London water' (devised by an American chemical manufacturer, Betz Laboratories) so that they could drink tea that tasted just like it did at home.

But, whatever water you use, tea-making is ultimately a matter of personal preference, from your favourite brand and most-beloved mug to your choice of accompanying biscuit.

Please don't write in.

· **CURIOSI-TEAS** ·

❯ In the complete collection of Agatha Christie's Miss Marple stories, the characters drink 143 cups of tea.

❯ The Guinness World Record for the most cups of tea made in one hour by a team of 12 is 1,848.

❯ In Chinese legend, the first tea plants sprouted from the eyelids of the founder of Zen, after he tore them off to punish himself for falling asleep during meditation.

Why and when did it become three meals a day?

Today, we generally eat three meals a day, but it wasn't always like this. The Romans actively frowned on the idea – they had an obsession with digestion and thought eating more than one meal a day was gluttonous. As a result, Romans often ate just one large meal around midday.

For most of the next 2,000 years, people ate two meals a day – dinner and supper. A 16th-century proverb said: 'To rise at six, dine at ten, sup at six and go to bed at ten, makes a man live ten times ten.' Sometimes a small snack was added in between, known as 'luncheon'. You would only take an extra meal earlier than 10 a.m. if you were ill, elderly or a worker who did a lot of manual labour – as you'd need an early-morning meal to help sustain you throughout the day. This was sometimes called 'breakfast', as it broke the fast that had begun the night before.

The Industrial Revolution created longer working hours for the majority of people, and three meals became the rule rather than the exception. 'Breakfast' kept its logical place as the name for the first meal, while 'dinner' was used for the midday meal, until 'luncheon' came into use in the south of England. 'Dinner' and 'supper' both became words for the third meal in the south, though the latter is more commonly used if the food is eaten later at night. Elsewhere 'dinner' remained the midday meal and 'tea' was the evening meal. To add to the confusion, artificial lighting meant that for more wealthy households in Britain, dinner/supper was often pushed later into the evening. The gap since lunch was now too long, resulting in a fourth meal called 'afternoon tea', which was shortened to 'teatime'.

So, to wrap up: dinner became lunch, supper became dinner, and breakfast and teatime were invented to fill in the gaps. All very confusing, and we haven't even touched on brunch, elevenses or midnight snacks.

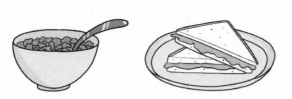

❯ 62% of Americans surveyed in 2019 would like 'second breakfast' to be an official meal.

❯ Until 1956, French schools were permitted to serve students under 14 up to half a litre of wine, cider or beer with a meal.

Why does orange juice taste so awful after you brush your teeth?

When you brushed your teeth this morning, did you notice how much foam you created? Perhaps it ended up splattered all over your chin, the sink and the bathroom mirror? That white froth is caused by a chemical in your toothpaste called sodium laureth sulphate (SLS). It makes liquids foam and bubble up, and you'll also find it in hand soap, washing-up liquid and floor cleaner. Delicious.

SLS is not only great at making bubbles; it is also cheap, non-toxic, odourless and has no taste of its own. But it can affect other flavours by suppressing your ability to taste sweet things and dissolving the fatty coating on your tongue that usually limits the sensation of bitterness. This means that when you reach for a glass of orange juice, you experience less of the sweetness from the sugar but more of the bitter citric acid, and together that creates the horrible flavour that is definitely *not* the best way to start your day.

········· **MOUTH-WATERING FACTS** ·········

❯ You may have learned in school that different parts of your tongue taste different flavours. This isn't true at all. Receptors for different tastes are spread all over your tongue.

❯ When Jelly Belly tried to make a cheese pizza-flavoured jelly bean, the result was so bad that they used it as the basis for their vomit-flavoured bean.

Why does less sleep make the skin around your eyes puffy and dark?

When we aren't properly rested, our body gives us a natural pick-me-up in the form of certain hormones, such as cortisol, which help to boost our energy levels and keep us awake and alert. One side effect of these hormones is that they make our blood vessels expand, and because the skin under our eyes is especially thin, all of that extra blood becomes visible and causes dark rings. The rings are easier to see in people with light skin. The extra hormones also cause our skin to hold more water, which is what causes puffiness around the eyes.

A lack of sleep can cause much bigger problems than puffy skin, though. Studies have shown that staying awake for between 17 and 19 hours impairs your physical and mental performance as much as being drunk. Tiredness has also been linked to depression, obesity, low IQ scores and feelings of loneliness.

The recommended amount of sleep for adults is between seven and nine hours a night, and it's impossible to overstate how important a good night's rest is. Sleeping well is beneficial for your immune system, your heart, your mental wellbeing, for regulating your appetite, managing your blood sugar levels, reducing the risk of Alzheimer's and even improving the efficiency of vaccinations. So if you're reading this book while propped up in bed at midnight, put it down and get some shut-eye.

Which fruit came first, the grape or the grapefruit?

The grape wins hands down.

Grapes have been around for almost 70 million years. The oldest fossilised grapes were found next to fragments of dinosaur eggs, suggesting dinosaurs may have eaten them. Grapefruit, on the other hand, are a very recent invention. King Henry VIII never had one for breakfast, and there are no grapefruit in the whole of Shakespeare. They didn't exist until the 18th century.

It's odd to think of a fruit being 'invented', but with citrus fruits it's quite common. Any kind can be crossed with any other to make a new one. At first, there were only three: the mandarin, the citron (like a lemon, with a thick rind) and the pomelo (the largest, up to 12 inches across). But citrus fruits love cross-pollinating – sometimes by chance, sometimes with the help of humans. And every new variety can combine with others in turn, to create yet more hybrids. So now there are thousands of kinds of citrus, from the familiar oranges, limes, clementines, satsumas, tangerines and kumquats to the less well-known etrogs, yuzus and chinottos . . . and, of course, the grapefruit.

Grapefruit were first seen in the Caribbean and were originally described in 1750 by Griffith Hughes, a Welsh vicar and amateur naturalist, who called them 'the forbidden fruit' of Barbados. No one seems to know why. They were a cross between the sweet orange of Jamaica and the huge green pomelo, which had been brought from the Spice Islands in Indonesia by a Captain Shaddock – hence the grapefruit's other name, 'the small shaddock'. Nobody knows if they came about naturally or whether Captain Shaddock had a hand in it.

So why are they called grapefruit, when they don't look or taste anything like grapes?

It's because of the way they grow on the tree, as first noted in 1820 by French botanist the Chevalier de Tussac, who observed that they hung down in bunches, or *grappes*, as he put it. A grapefruit should really be a 'group-fruit'.

ORANGE + Pomelo = GRApefruit!

· **FRUITY FACTS** ·

❯ The French for 'grapefruit' is *pamplemousse*, which comes from a combination of Dutch and Portuguese and means 'pumpkin-lemon'.

❯ A blue whale can't swallow anything larger than a grapefruit.

❯ The chemical that gives grapefruit its distinctive taste is called nootkatone. In spray form it's an excellent insecticide and mosquito repellent.

Why do we eat mouldy cheese but not mouldy bread?

Mould is a type of fungus, and just like its brethren, mushrooms, some moulds are good for you, while some need to be avoided at all costs. Penicillin is a mould, for example, and a member of the penicillin family is used to make Brie and Camembert. It gives them their distinctive flavours, forms their firm, furry rinds, and its antibiotic properties kill off harmful bacteria within the cheese.

Moulds are also sometimes added to cheese to change its chemistry, so it becomes creamier, or crumblier, or tastier, or blue, or green. They do this with chemicals called 'enzymes', which get their name from the Greek word meaning 'in yeast'.

The word 'yeast', meanwhile, comes from the Old English term for 'froth'. It's what makes bread rise. It's also a type of fungus, so while fresh bread doesn't (or shouldn't) contain mould, it would be very flat if it wasn't for fungi.

Many different types of mould can grow on bread. Some are safe to eat, some are not, but it's impossible to tell which is which without a microscope. So it's best not to eat mouldy bread at all. And it's not really a good idea to just scrape it off, because fungus has roots, which are less easy to see and remove, so you might end up eating them.

Cheese is different. If unwanted mould appears on a cheese like Cheddar, it's okay to cut it out. Hard cheese is much less porous than bread, so the roots cannot grow very deep.

Who knew a cheese sandwich could be so complicated?

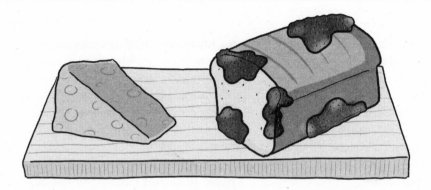

❯ Sodium citrate is used in the production of nacho cheese and has the chemical formula $Na_3C_6H_5O_7$.

❯ 'Tyromancy' is the act of predicting the future by observing the coagulation of cheese.

❯ In 1966, a US patent was issued for a cheese-flavoured cigarette.

❯ In 1813, Camembert cheese was made an honorary citizen of the town of Caen in Normandy.

Why is bacon the only meat that comes in rashers?

Quite simply, a 'rasher' is a thin slice of meat cooked by grilling, frying or broiling. The reason we associate the word with bacon is that it's the meat that we most commonly cook that way. But the word used to mean any sliced food. A play from the 1630s mentions 'a cherry-tart cut into rashers', and in the 1890s you could be offered a 'rasher of watermelon'.

The most likely origin of the word is from the Middle English *rash*, meaning 'to cut'. There was a suggestion it was because the meat had to be cooked quickly, or 'rashly', but this theory has now fallen out of fashion.

The opposite of a rasher is a 'flitch' – a huge chunk of bacon. This used to mean any kind of meat, but today it's only pork. There's a tradition in the Essex town of Great Dunmow that if you can prove that you and your spouse haven't argued for over a year, then you win a flitch of bacon. However, competing couples are cross-examined by a judge and jury to test their claims, so it's a lot of work just for a side of bacon.

What is broiling?

If you grill something, you apply a heat source from below, like on a barbecue. Broiling is when you apply the heat from above. Confusingly, this function on ovens is called 'grill', but technically it should be 'broil'.

❯ In 2018, Ohio State University installed a vending machine that sold only bacon.

❯ The world's oldest cat (named Crème Puff) lived to be 38. Her owner speculates that her long life was due to her unusual diet: bacon, eggs and coffee with heavy cream.

❯ In one of Brighton's cemeteries, there is a Robert Bacon buried next to a Florence Egg.

❯ In 2013, an American food company launched a bacon-scented deodorant 'for people who sweat like pigs'.

Why do we have an overbite?

Most humans have a slight overbite. Our top front teeth hang over the ones at the bottom when we close our mouths. We used to have an edge-to-edge bite, with the tips of our top and bottom teeth meeting squarely. An American anthropologist, the aptly named Charles Loring Brace, put forward a theory that this change was due to the adoption of cutlery.

Brace pointed out that before we started cutting up our food, we'd use our incisors to clamp it in the mouth and rip it. This eating method, he reasoned, would naturally lead to teeth that matched together all the way round. Once people started using cutlery to do all the cutting work, the incisors would no longer be worn down, and the top layer of teeth would keep on 'erupting' from the gum. As they ran out of space to grow, they would be forced forward, eventually leading to a permanent overbite.

Brace studied hundreds of skulls to see if the placement of their teeth matched his theory. Cutlery became widespread in America several decades after it did in Europe, and he found that the majority of American skulls retained their edge-to-edge bite for longer than those of Europeans. He also found that Chinese aristocrats developed an overbite roughly 1,000 years before people in Europe. This might be because they were using chopsticks, which requires pre-cut food.

We can't be certain that Brace's theory is correct; for example, not all food needs to be 'clamped' in the mouth, and if you ate mostly soft foods, then you wouldn't use your incisors much. While the idea that our use of cutlery changed our anatomy is interesting, the evidence isn't definitive, so it's worth taking this theory with a pinch of salt.

What is the origin of the word 'gaff' when referring to your home?

The first use of the word 'gaff' in reference to a location came in 1753, when it was a slang term for a fair. We're not sure where the word came from, but the two best theories are that it comes from the Romani word *gav*, meaning 'town', or that it refers to the 'gabbling' noises you might hear at a funfair.

Wherever it originated, the word's meaning later expanded to include other places where you could find public amusement, such as music halls. In the 1930s, it evolved again to include shops, businesses or people's homes, which is when we started inviting people round to our 'gaffs'. We like to think it's because you're hoping to offer them a good time – or, indeed, all the fun of the fair.

····················· ORIGIN STORIES ·····················

❯ The word 'scientist' was coined in 1834 to describe Mary Somerville – not only because of the inappropriateness of the term 'man of science', but also because her work covered so many fields, including mathematics, physics and geology.

❯ The political terms 'left wing' and 'right wing' were established in 18th-century France, when progressive politicians would sit to the left of the president and conservative politicians to the right.

Why is plastic called 'plastic'?

'Plastic' comes from the ancient Greek word *plastikos*, meaning 'able to be formed or shaped'. In that sense, many natural materials are 'plastic', including clay, wax, wood, bronze, ivory and marble. The word also referred to a sculptor, and so Michelangelo might have called himself a *plasticatore*.

The first man-made plastic material was patented in 1856 by Alexander Parkes, a metallurgist from Birmingham whose great-uncle, Samuel, had invented the key ring. From castor oil and chloroform he made a substance as 'hard as horn, but as flexible as leather', which he called Parkesine.

Parkes went broke, but in 1869 his partner, Daniel Spill, patented Xylonite, from *xylon*, Greek for 'wood'. Xylonite was used to make jewellery boxes, combs and washable detachable shirt collars. However, over in America there was a rival bursting onto the plastic scene.

He was a New Yorker named John Wesley Hyatt, who'd invented a very similar material, which he called celluloid. In 1863, he'd set out to win a $10,000 prize that would be awarded to whoever found a new way to make billiard balls, which at the time were made of ivory. They weren't cheap: you could only get four or five out of one tusk. After six years, Hyatt patented celluloid, hailing himself as 'saviour of the elephant'. His new balls weren't a success, however. They caught fire if a cigar touched them and, when hit hard, exploded with a sharp crack, making every man in the billiard hall reach for his gun. Hyatt also tried making celluloid false teeth, but they were similarly unsuccessful. Today the material is mainly used for ping-pong balls and guitar picks.

The next breakthrough came in New York in 1907. A

Belgian chemist called Leo Baekeland had combined two chemicals to make polyoxybenzylmethylenglycolanhydride. For five years, he exposed it to heat and pressure in what he called a 'bakelizer'. The end result was the much more catchy Bakelite. It had three big pluses over Parkesine, Xylonite and celluloid: it was easy to mass-produce, it didn't conduct electricity and it didn't burst into flames – perfect for lamps, radios and telephones. By the time Baekeland died in 1944, Bakelite had 15,000 different uses.

During all this, there were endless legal squabbles over who had invented what first and who had thought of the various names. But everyone agreed they were all 'plastic' materials (or 'plastics' for short), and so plastic is what we ended up calling them.

If plastic bags and bottles had been invented 400 years ago (at the same time as the word 'plastic'), used and then thrown away (by, say, Oliver Cromwell), they still wouldn't have fully biodegraded. Today 99% of all plastic is made from fossil fuels, and half of all plastic is used only once before it goes to landfill. The strength and durability that makes it so useful also makes it hard to dispose of.

· **PLASTIC FANTASTIC** ·

❯ In Socrates' time, a *plastikarios* was a potter.

❯ Most of us consume about five grams of plastic in our food and drink every week. That's about a credit card's worth.

❯ The University of Maine has created biodegradable golf balls out of crushed lobster shells so that people can play golf on cruise ships.

Why do scones have cream on the bottom and jam on top in Devon, but it's the other way round in Cornwall?

This is quite the debate. The earliest known reference to cream tea dates back to AD 997 and it comes from Devon, not Cornwall. Ordulf, the Earl of Devon, was said to have rewarded his labourers with a combination of bread, clotted cream and strawberry preserves. Unfortunately, the ancient manuscripts fail to provide details of whether he served his cream teas with the jam or the cream on top.

The crux of the argument seems to be that Devonians see cream as an under-layer, like butter. Over in Cornwall, however, they see it as a topping, like the frosting on a cake. The joke in Cornwall is that the Cornish cream sits on top because they're proud of it, whereas Devonians are slightly ashamed of theirs, so they cover it up with jam.

The Cornish are so proud of their clotted cream that it has received a Protected Designation of Origin (PDO) classification, like champagne, which means it can only be produced in a specific region and in a specific manner: with milk produced in Cornwall, and with a fat content of over 55%. A similar campaign was launched for the 'Devon Cream Tea' in 2010, the application for which included the 'correct' order of toppings, but it was unsuccessful.

However, when the royal family posted a photo of their cream tea on Instagram in 2020, the scones were clearly prepared the Devon way. What the Duke and Duchess of Cornwall thought about the matter was not recorded.

Why does cat food come in beef and lamb flavours, but not mouse?

Cats were domesticated around 12,000 years ago, and for most of their time as pets they were largely kept outdoors. Farmers used them for pest control: to hunt mice and small animals that might eat stored grains, an activity that was already second nature and a means of survival when they were wild. They still have this instinct, of course, but when a house cat catches a mouse today, it is just a bonus mid-morning snack.

Some people think that we should still be giving cats a fully mouse-based diet. They are fans of 'Biologically Appropriate Raw Feeding', or BARF. (It's sometimes also called the 'Bones and Raw Food' diet, which makes us think that they decided on the acronym before deciding what it stood for.) The idea is that since cats catch and eat mice in the wild (and don't catch and eat cows very often), it's unnatural to give them foods such as beef.

The main problem is one of economics. Each mouse provides only a small amount of meat, and to scale that up to millions of tins of cat food would take a lot of mouse-farming, whereas cows and sheep are already widely reared and commercially available, and just a small percentage of the animal is needed to fill up a pouch of food. Also, the idea of opening a pouch of mouse meat to give to your kitten is enough to make you BARF.

····················· PAWS FOR THOUGHT ····················

❭ A group of wild cats is called a 'destruction'.

Why do we say 'blowing raspberries'?

It's rhyming slang. A 'raspberry tart' is a fart.

❯ The word 'grass', meaning someone who informs to the police, comes from 'grasshopper', cockney rhyming slang for 'copper'.

❯ If you're alone, you're 'on your tod', because 'alone' rhymes with Tod Sloan, a famous American jockey from the late 19th century.

❯ Other cockney rhyming words and phrases include 'tomfoolery' (jewellery), 'Cadbury's Flake' (mistake) and 'brass tacks' (facts).

❯ Lots of rhyming slang relates to places in London, such as 'Barnet' for hair, which is taken from Barnet Fair.

Do birds fly faster if they fart?

While it would be fun to hear a flock of flatulence-fuelled flamingos in flight, birds don't actually fart. Nobody is quite sure why. One theory is that food doesn't spend long enough in their system to ferment and produce farts. Or it could be that gas continually leaks out of a bird instead of being stored up for a big eruption.

Birds also can't swallow. They don't have the muscles to push food down their throat, so have to rely on gravity to move it downwards. Birds can vomit, however, and – just to cover the full gamut of avian excretions – they also poo, of course, although bird poo isn't white – that's bird pee. The pee and poo come out of the same hole – the dark bit in the middle is the poo – though both are equally annoying if they land on your windscreen.

······················· **FARTY FACTS** ······················

❯ When threatened, Sonoran coral snakes fart at their enemies.

❯ Termites fart a lot: they produce up to 5% of global methane emissions each year.

Why do birds fly in a 'V' formation?

Flying in a 'V' is hard work for the bird at the front, but much easier for the other birds. That's because each one flies slightly higher than the bird in front of it, which creates a slight updraught with each flap of its wings. The birds can use this little bit of extra wind to glide for a second, and over a long journey that results in far fewer flaps. Birds take it in turns at the front, so nobody gets too tired. Better still, if they're in a 'V', each bird can keep a close eye on the one in front of it, and the bird behind can watch the one in front, and so on, helping to keep the whole flock in check.

It's just a much better way of getting around. The question should be: why don't all birds fly that way?

Okay, so why don't all birds fly in a 'V' formation?

Some birds fly alone. This could be because they're not particularly social animals, or because they don't need the help. If they have particularly big wings, like a falcon, they can use the natural air currents to keep themselves aloft and don't need to rely on their friends for a bit of updraught. Other birds prefer to fly in a huge flock, the idea being that since there are many of them, they stand a better chance against predators.

· · · · · · · · · · · · · · · · · · · IN-FORMATION · · · · · · · · · · · · · · · · · · ·

❯ Migratory birds can 'sleep-fly' while undertaking long flights.

❯ Birds that are better at flying have pointier eggs.

Do penguins drink salt water?

It's difficult for penguins to avoid drinking salt water, given that most of their meals are eaten beneath the surface of the ocean. However, thanks to an inbuilt filtering system located next to their eyes known as the supraorbital gland, the salt doesn't stay inside them very long. The salty water they drink enters their bloodstream, but as the blood passes through that gland, the salt gets collected like tea leaves in a strainer, stopping it from making its way through to the rest of their body. Once a penguin has collected all that salt, they will either sneeze it back out or let it slowly dribble out of their nose.

The supraorbital gland isn't their only incredible gland; at the other end of the penguin you'll find the preen gland. Located by their bottom, it produces waterproofing oil that spreads across their feathers to provide insulation and reduce friction in water.

Without their feathers, they are not waterproof, so rather than constantly replacing them like most birds, they squash the entire process into a two-week period known as a 'catastrophic moult', during which every single feather is replaced with a new one. Penguins can also triple their swimming speed by releasing air bubbles from their feathers, allowing them to launch out of the ocean, into the air and onto ice shelves. And male king penguins can store undigested food in their stomachs for up to three weeks by switching on a preservative function that effectively turns them into a freezer.

· **A PROJECTILE FACT** ·

❯ Some penguins generate a rectal pressure that is strong enough to propel their excrement over a metre away from their nest.

If baby kangaroos live in their mother's pouch, where do they poo?

Human parents will empathise: children can be messy. While we might have to tidy empty crisp packets and rogue LEGO bricks from a child's bedroom, for a kangaroo mother it's urine and poo they need to clean, and the room in question is their own pouch. Their short arms are not really up to the job, so they have to do most of the work with their tongue.

It's not quite as bad as it sounds. Baby kangaroos only produce a tiny droplet of waste at a time, and they are surprisingly well potty-trained. They can't go unless they're being licked by their mother, which means she can control the process – and they can even pass the waste directly onto her tongue. It's just as well, as it means the poo won't congregate in those 'hard-to-clean' corners.

Koalas also keep their babies in pouches, but they don't have the benefit of a kangaroo's long snout and tongue to lick themselves clean. Instead, koala pouches have a clever self-cleaning mechanism. When the joey is ready to leave, the mother secretes an anti-bacterial liquid that dries into a crusty powder, leaving the pouch completely sterile for the next baby. Beats tackling a teenager's room with a mop and bucket any day.

························· **A ROO-LLY GOOD FACT** ···················

❯ Ernest Hemingway was part kangaroo. After he was in a car accident, he had his bones bound together with kangaroo tendon.

Why are dusters almost always yellow?

Let's come clean: we don't know for sure. Here are our favourite theories:

Trousers
The 18th-century version of blue jeans was yellow nankeen breeches. These trousers, made from naturally occurring yellow cotton, were extremely popular, and so when people wanted to make dusters, they would often just rip up an old pair of nankeens. The name comes from 'Nankin', an old British name for the Chinese city of Nanjing, where the fabric was made. When dusters were made commercially, yellow was already associated with household cleaning.

Butter
When butter is made, it is passed through muslin, a process that stains the cloth yellow. And when these cloths were no longer usable in the dairy, they'd be turned into dusters. Again, the colour became linked with cleaning, so manufacturers made their new cloths yellow to match.

Quarantine
When ships came into port, they would fly a yellow flag to show they needed a quarantine inspection. This link to hygiene may explain why dusters are yellow, but it seems a bit less likely, as a cloth that is yellow, signalling potential disease, doesn't seem particularly appealing as a household cleaner.

It could simply be that yellow is a cheerful colour which shows up dirt clearly. That, at least, is a tidy explanation.

Why do we itch?

Some itches happen because your skin feels something touching it and a message is sent to your brain that you might be under threat. The resulting scratch is the easiest way to dislodge something dangerous, whether it's the tendrils of a poisonous plant, biting insects like bedbugs or lice, or a venomous spider. In actual fact, the thing touching you is almost certainly not trying to hurt you, but the body has a strict 'better safe than sorry' policy.

Other itches are caused by the presence of a toxin or foreign substance, such as saliva from an insect. When a mosquito decides to snack on us, our bodies recognise their spit as a potentially harmful foreign agent and deploy a chemical called histamine to fight it off. The histamine floods the area with extra blood and defensive white blood cells, but it also stimulates the nerves around the bite, leading to an itching sensation.

You may have noticed that sometimes just seeing someone else scratch is enough to make you itchy. This makes sense from a survival perspective: the fact that someone nearby is feeling itchy suggests there might be parasites around, so we instinctively start scratching to get rid of them.

You don't even need to see someone scratching to feel itchy; sometimes just reading about a subject like bedbugs or lice is enough to get you going. If you're feeling itchy now, it's probably our fault. Sorry about that.

········· **AN UP-TO-SCRATCH FACT** ·········

❯ Scratchy Bottom is a valley in Dorset.

How does scratch and sniff work?

To begin with, scented oil is mixed with liquid plastic for twelve hours, by which time both have been minced into droplets so tiny that they are invisible to the naked eye. Then a chemical is added which causes the plastic molecules to seal themselves up, and as they do so, each one captures a droplet of oil. These sealed balls – called 'microcapsules' – can then be glued to a piece of paper, so you effectively have a million minuscule perfume bottles stuck to the page. When you scratch the paper, the 'bottles' break, releasing the scented oil molecules, and suddenly you can smell raspberry.

Or gas. In 1987, Baltimore Gas and Electric sent customers a scratch-and-sniff sticker to warn them what natural gas smelt like. Unfortunately, the journey caused many of the microcapsules to break, the smell of gas leaked out, and the company had to deal with several hundred false alarms.

· · · · · · · · · · · · · · · **FACTS NOT TO BE SNIFFED AT** · · · · · · · · · · · · · · ·

❯ In 2013, the charity Crimestoppers sent marijuana-scented scratch-and-sniff cards to thousands of homes, to help people detect the smell of illegal cannabis farms.

❯ In 1981, film director John Waters released a movie called *Polyester*, which had a numbered scratch-and-sniff guide so that you could smell the movie as you watched it. Smells included pizza, glue and human poo.

Why do I have so many odd socks?

The Sock Loss Formula was devised in 2016 by psychologist Dr Simon Moore and statistician Dr Geoff Ellis. They factored in laundry size (L), washing complexity (C), positivity towards doing laundry (P) and degree of attention while doing it (A).

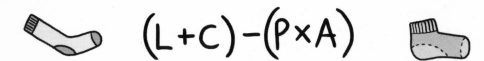

$$(L+C)-(P \times A)$$

They surmise that if you're not giving the task your undivided attention, you'll lose 15 socks a year, more or less (or as they might put it, Moore–Ellis).

Socks have such a bad reputation for disappearing because they are the only clothes in your laundry that come in sets of two; you'd probably lose your pants too, if they consisted of two halves. In fact, you probably *are* losing your pants, and various other bits of clothing, but they haven't got a twin to let you know the other one is missing.

Likely places you might find stray socks include beneath a sofa cushion, behind the radiator, tucked at the very back of your drawer, or wherever your pet sleeps. Unlikely places? Free inside a cereal box.

One way to save yourself the hassle is to buy all your socks in the same colour, so every sock can be twinned with every other sock. Or you could stop wearing them all together. Einstein never did, not even when the president invited him to the White House. He gave up on socks because his big toes kept poking holes in them. Which is odd, because in physics TOE stands for Theory Of Everything.

And Einstein spent his whole life searching for his big TOE.

· **SOCK AND AWE** ·

❯ In 2014, a Great Dane ate 43½ socks and survived.

❯ In 2019, Longleat safari park was inundated with socks gifted from around the world, following their appeal for help in keeping their chipmunk family warm during winter.

❯ The stocking shortage in post-Second World War America triggered a series of events now known as 'the nylon riots'.

Why does a mirror spin you around but not flip you upside down?

. . . .

Turn this book around to face the nearest mirror and try to read the text. It will all be going in the wrong direction, from right to left. Or, if you're reading this in Arabic or Urdu, from left to right.

(You can turn the book back around to face you now.)

Similarly, if you raise your right hand, your reflection raises its left hand. It looks like the mirror has switched you from left to right without flipping your top and bottom, but in fact it's done neither. When you followed the instruction at the start of this entry, it was *you* who turned the image around before pointing it at the mirror. If, instead, you had written something on transparent glass and held it up to a mirror without turning it around, it would have been perfectly legible (depending on your handwriting).

What mirrors *do* do is reverse an image from back to front. It's as if your face was a rubber mask, and as that mask hits the reflective surface, it's pulled inside out by it. So what you're seeing when you look at your reflection is an inside-out version of the surface of your face.

If you want a mirror to turn you upside down, take it off the wall, lay it on the floor and stand on it very carefully. Like a mountain that appears upside down in the surface of a lake, you're now being pulled inside out from top to bottom, because the mirror's surface is touching the bottom of you. Don't be tempted to jump up and down.

That would be seven years' bad luck.

Can animals recognise their reflections?

Dolphins, chimpanzees and magpies can all recognise themselves in a mirror, and the latest discovery is that cleaner wrasse fish can do it too. When they were placed in mirrored tanks with dots drawn on their heads, as soon as the fish spotted the dots, they tried to get them off by rubbing their heads against hard surfaces.

· A FLIPPING GOOD FACT ·

❯ Leonardo da Vinci wrote all his notes backwards and in mirror writing, probably because he was left-handed and didn't want to smudge the ink.

❯ Leonardo da Vinci wrote all his notes backwards and in mirror writing, probably because he was left-handed and didn't want to smudge the ink.

What's on the other side of my belly button?

Your belly button is a scar caused by the cutting of the umbilical cord, which carried nutrients and oxygen to you from your mother's placenta before you were born. After birth, it was snipped off and the part on the outside shrivelled away, leaving a belly button, but the bit inside kept working. In fact, it's still working now.

Some of the veins and arteries that were connected to your mother now supply blood to your bladder. Others sealed up after birth and were repurposed as the ligaments that divide your liver into different sections. If you prod your belly button, you can sometimes feel a tingling in your pelvic area: that's because it's still directly linked to the network of blood vessels and tissues inside your body.

Belly buttons are curious things. In 2011, the Belly Button Biodiversity Project examined swabs from the navels of 60 people and found 2,368 different species of bacteria, over half of which may have been completely new to science. One man's navel contained a bacterium that was known to exist only in Japanese soil, even though he had never been to Japan. Who knows what mysteries may be hiding in yours?

······················· **EXTRA FLUFF** ·······················

❯ An Australian man holds the Guinness World Record for his collection of belly-button fluff. He's been saving it for 26 years and has 22.1 grams' worth.

Where do the words 'left' and 'right' come from, and is it a coincidence that 'right' means 'correct'?

You're right that 'right' and 'right' are connected. It's because 'right' was considered right. Right?

The words 'right' and 'left' date back at least 800 years. 'Right' is from the Old English word *riht*, which meant 'good' or 'proper'. 'Left', by contrast, comes from the word *lyft*, which meant 'weak'. It's due to handedness: the right hand was seen as the 'correct' hand to use because for the 90% of people who are right-handed that one is stronger.

Whether you are a rightie or a leftie is down to genetics, and your preference is shown early. Babies in the womb already have a preference for which thumb to suck, which continues after they're born.

One in a hundred people are ambidextrous and can use either hand with equal ability. The word comes from the Latin for 'both correct', though its original meaning was very different: it meant someone who took bribes from both sides in a legal case.

Dogs can be right- or left-pawed, elephants are right- or left-trunked depending on the side to which they prefer to twist their trunks, and apes are divided 50/50 into righties and lefties.

· **A LEFTIE FACT** ·

❯ Famous lefties include Paul McCartney, Oprah Winfrey, Judy Garland, Lady Gaga, Barack Obama and Bart Simpson.

Why does red mean 'stop' and green mean 'go'?

Red is the colour of danger and bloodshed. The Romans associated it with Mars, the god of war, for Christians it is linked with the devil, and when pirates wanted to let other ships know that they would fight without mercy, they raised a red flag.

In 1841, during the early days of train travel, senior British railway managers held a meeting to decide which colours to use for railway signals. They chose red for 'stop', green for 'proceed with caution' and white for 'go'. However, in 1876, after a stroke of bad luck when a red lens fell from its holder, leaving the white light behind it exposed, a serious crash occurred. After that, the rail company changed its signals to green for 'go' and yellow for 'caution', since these two colours were distinct from each other, and from red.

In 1868, the world's first traffic light was introduced on the road outside the Houses of Parliament in London to help deal with the growing number of horse-drawn carriages. It used a flag system during the day and gas lights at night, with red for 'stop' and green for 'caution'. After less than a month, the traffic light exploded due to a gas leak, injuring the policeman operating it. The project was shelved, but the precedent for red and green lights on British roads had been set.

In early-20th-century America, each state had a different system for controlling traffic: some had red and green lights, some had signals that read 'Stop' and 'Go', and some used bells and buzzers to indicate when a light was about to change. For a period in 1920s New York, green meant 'stop' on roads going east to west and 'go' on those going north to south. But common sense prevailed and everyone got behind a system that had been developed in Detroit and was based on the railways. It used the three colours – green, amber and red – that we still use today.

. . . .

Why are normal cars able to go so fast, when the maximum speed limit means you'll never actually drive at that speed? A car with a more powerful engine can accelerate faster, carry heavier loads and go up steeper hills. It can also move at a higher speed. You can't really have the first three desirable things without the rather pointless last one. It is possible to install speed limiters, but they waste a lot of fuel and are of no use in cars that are sold in different countries, each of which may have a different maximum speed limit. Manufacturers also know that some customers prefer to buy a car that can reach 150 mph instead of 140 mph, even if they're never going to go that fast.

. . . . **GREEN-LIT FACTS** . . . .

❯ Historically, Japan didn't have separate words for blue and green, which has had confusing knock-on effects. Some Japanese traffic lights appear blue, but officials will insist that they're green.

❯ During the Cultural Revolution in China, some of the Red Guards wanted to make red mean 'go' and green mean 'stop', but they decided against it on safety grounds.

❯ Some traffic lights in Mumbai won't switch to green unless cars stop honking their horns.

Why are British car number plates white at the front and yellow at the back?

So other drivers can tell whether you're coming or going.

❯ The Queen is the only person who doesn't need a licence plate.

❯ The DVLA keeps a list of rude licence plates that are banned; e.g. SN07 is forbidden because it looks like SNOT.

❯ The most expensive plate sold in the UK was 25 O. It went for over £500,000 pounds because the buyer wanted to put it on his Ferrari 250.

When a motorway sign says
LONDON - 50 MILES ⟩⟩ where exactly is it 50 miles from?

Traditionally, all distance markers for London referred to a large cross erected in memory of Eleanor of Castile, the wife of Edward I. When she died in 1290, the King had her body taken from the embalmers in Lincoln to her burial place in London. At every spot the body stopped, a cross was erected. The final and most elaborate one was on what is now a roundabout on the southern edge of Trafalgar Square.

Anti-monarchists demolished the cross during the English Civil War, and so signs to London referred to the empty spot where the monument had once stood. However, in 1675 a statue of Charles I, which had survived the war, was erected in its place. A replica of the Eleanor Cross was built in the 19th century and placed down the road, just outside Charing Cross station, but the statue of Charles remains London's point zero to this day. Not all British towns have a statue of Charles I or a monument to Eleanor of Castile to measure from, and landmarks vary from place to place. Some distance markers refer to marketplaces or civic buildings, and Highways England – the body responsible for England's road signage – say they usually choose somewhere that is simply 'appropriate for drivers'.

Google Maps uses the geometry of a town, calculates the shape of the place and puts a pin in its exact centre. This gives some interesting results: according to Google, the centre of Newcastle is a nondescript café owned and run by the city's university.

What is the furthest, straightest distance you can walk on Earth?

It is possible to walk in a straight line all the way from Sagres, on the south coast of Portugal, to Jinjiang, in the far east of China. That's 6,984 miles. Luckily, Jinjiang is famous for being the sports shoe capital of China, so when you arrive, you can get fitted out with a new pair of trainers before you start the walk back.

···················· RAMBLING FACTS ····················

❯ Blindfolded people walk around in circles, even when they think they're walking in a straight line.

❯ On the US mainland, the furthest you can be, in a straight line, from a McDonald's is 120 miles.

When does a rock become an island?

Drawing up exact rules to define an island is tricky. The EU, for instance, excludes land masses that are less than a kilometre from the mainland; are attached to the mainland by a rigid structure; have fewer than 50 permanent residents; or are home to the capital of an EU state. Under these rules Great Britain, Anglesey, Skye and Lundy are not islands. Do you want to break it to them or shall we?

Much simpler is an old Scottish rule that 'if a piece of land will support a sheep, it's an island. If not, it's a rock.' The UN takes that a step further: in 2016, its Permanent Court of Arbitration said that the difference between a rock and an island is that the latter can support human life.

The world's smallest island by those rules is in the St Lawrence River, between New York and Ontario, and is called Just Room Enough. It's the size of a tennis court and contains just one house, one tree and a small patch of beach. The owners built the house to find peace and quiet, but because it is so unusual, it has become a tourist attraction, with boats full of sightseers going past to take a look.

Is Bishop Rock an island or a rock?

Bishop Rock, in the Isles of Scilly, is 46 metres long and home to one of Britain's tallest lighthouses. It used to be regarded by the *Guinness Book of Records* as the world's smallest island to have a building on it. However, the lighthouse was automated in 1982, so with no people living there it has now been reclassified as a rock.

Aargh, me hearties! Why do pirates be speakin' like this?

Robert Louis Stevenson's *Treasure Island* begins in Bristol, where the one-legged seafarer Long John Silver owns a pub. In the 1950 film adaptation of the book, English actor Robert Newton played the world's most famous swashbuckler, and his gruff West Country accent (and a penchant for overacting) resulted in the stereotypical pirate that we know today.

The nine 'aargh' noises that punctuated his speeches in the film were all his own creation. When he appeared in the sequel, he managed 27 'aarghs'. And as the title character in *Blackbeard the Pirate* (1952), he said 'aargh' at least 50 times.

While some real-life pirates did come from the West Country, most came from elsewhere, including London, Ireland, France and Spain. So if it wasn't for Stevenson and Newton, we would have no reason to think of a West Country accent as the 'standard' way for pirates to talk. The truth is, we don't know how pirates actually spoke at all, because they didn't write much down.

········· **BOOTY-FUL FACTS** ·········

❯ According to *The Pirate Primer: Mastering the Language of Swashbucklers and Rogues*, the word 'aargh' has 44 different possible meanings when used by an on-screen pirate.

❯ The pirate Benjamin Hornigold once attacked a ship in order to steal the hats of everyone on board, because his crew had got drunk and thrown their own overboard.

When should I use a semicolon?

The most common use of a semicolon is when the writer wants to link two separate but related ideas in the same sentence. The semicolon replaces a full stop or conjunction (e.g. 'such as', 'and', 'because', 'so'). For example, you could say:

I've just started reading this entry, but I already regret my decision.

Or:

I've just started reading this entry; I already regret my decision.

They are also useful when separating out a list. The semicolon helps to make things clearer when the list is lengthy and already contains commas. Like so:

There are many different entries in this book: the historical ones, which will appeal to daydreamers; the etymological ones, which will appeal to bookworms; and this grammatical one, which will appeal to almost no one, but it's important, so we're keeping it in, all right?

A third, and final, use (we're sad it's nearly over too) is when your sentence includes a conjunctive adverb (e.g. 'furthermore', 'however', 'thus'):

I have finished reading this entry; therefore, I can go out into the world and bask in the glory of my newly discovered semicolon knowledge. I'm certain I will make new friends because of it.

And it's as simple as that.

Have I read this page before?

The first person to give an explanation for déjà vu – the spooky feeling that something seems oddly familiar – was St Augustine of Hippo. Augustine is the patron saint of brewers, because he lived a life of debauchery and partying before giving it all up to become a monk. He thought déjà vu was caused by 'deceitful spirits' who were trying to sow confusion. Perhaps this was because, for him, any flashbacks might be related to his sinful past.

The phrase 'déjà vu', which translates as 'already seen', was coined by the 19th-century French philosopher Émile Boirac, who was the president of Dijon University but spent most of his time doing experiments on clairvoyance and mysticism. He believed déjà vu was due to emotions, and thought that if you have the same emotional feelings in two different situations then your mind might accidentally confuse the two.

Déjà vu is still a bit of a mystery, but the current best theory is that it's your brain doing a quick memory stock-check. When you're in a situation that is similar to one you've experienced in the past, your brain gets confused and sends signals of familiarity, along with a feeling of slight unease. Researchers say that it's a good sign, indicating that your faculties are in full working order, which could explain why it's more common in younger people, who tend to have a better memory.

Perhaps you're revisiting this page in the full knowledge that you've read it before. Studies show that people often enjoy watching TV shows, films and books more, or in a different way, the second time around. But you knew that already.

Are there different sign languages for deaf people from different countries?

Yes. In fact, there are more forms of sign language than there are countries in the world.

Nicaraguan sign language is one of them – the first new language in the history of the world to have been entirely invented by children.

Nicaragua is the second-poorest country in the western hemisphere, and for most of the 20th century it was a dictatorship. The only two special education schools it had were private, and deaf children were isolated at home with their families.

This all changed in 1979, when a new revolutionary government seized power and began a widespread programme of public education. As no qualified sign-language teachers were available, deaf children were taught Spanish and lip-reading. To the disappointment of parents and teachers, they struggled in class. In the playground, however, and on the school bus and the football field, they started creating their very own sign language. It caught on rapidly, evolving its own vocabulary and even its own grammar, using almost no words or signs from any other language.

People have been using hand gestures to express themselves since humanity began. The first actual sign language was developed in Benedictine monasteries so that the brothers didn't have to break their vows of silence. In the mid-1500s, one of them, a monk called Dom Pedro Ponce de León, realised it could be adapted to help people with hearing difficulties, and so he started a school. By the 1700s, there were schools for the deaf in both Britain and France, but their sign languages were totally different.

The first American school for the deaf opened in 1817. Two years before, its founder had been on a study tour of Europe, where the British had been very stand-offish, but the French had been willing to share everything. As a result, speakers of American Sign Language today can get along fine with the French but not the English.

There are 193 countries in the world and over 300 different sign languages. The Swiss and Mexican systems evolved from the French one; those in New Zealand and Northern Ireland from British Sign Language. Others, like Venezuelan and Turkish Sign Language, evolved completely independently.

Just as with the spoken word, multiple dialects and languages are often used in the same country. In Spain, about a quarter of the words signed in Valencia or Catalonia aren't used at all in official Spanish Sign Language. And in rare cases where signers grow up using one language and then learn another, they even have an 'accent'.

. . . .

How do deaf people from different countries communicate?
This was discussed at the first World Deaf Congress in Rome in 1951, and developed into something called Gestuno, combining the ideas of 'gesture' and 'oneness'. But when it was unveiled at the World Federation of the Deaf Congress in Bulgaria in 1976, the delegates found it completely incomprehensible. Today, a system called International Sign is used for conferences, events and games, but it still doesn't really count as a proper language and a lot of creative improvisation goes on.

Why can't I draw?

You can. Everybody can draw. Whether or not you get good at it is totally up to you.

You might think you don't have natural talent, but hard work is vital too. A 1993 study of violinists found that you could tell who were the top-ranked musicians simply by looking at how much they had practised. The average amount of practice time required to get to the top was 10,000 hours, but those hours were not spent simply 'doing'; the musicians had a purpose, a goal and a teacher. We never said it would be easy.

Of course, there are artists who are born with a gift. Pablo Picasso's drawings might appear to be simplistic at times, but as he once said when visiting an exhibition of children's drawings: 'When I was their age I could draw like Raphael. It took me a lifetime to draw like them.' This is borne out by a masterful self-portrait created when Picasso was just 15 years old that can be seen in the Picasso Museum in Barcelona.

But it's not just about raw talent. As a teenager in rural Japan, Yayoi Kusama, now known for her polka-dot pumpkins and light installations, started exhibiting in group shows. She was given no encouragement by her family, and as a woman in mid-20th-century Japan, societal norms were against her. But neither problem could suppress her wish to become the artist she knew she could be, and today her works are displayed around the world and are sold for more money than any other living female artist's. She had talent, of course, but she had determination too.

At some point, everyone, no matter what level they're at, needs to learn from someone or be inspired by something.

That's how artists grow and improve. A teacher might say that drawing is about looking, and this means *really* looking. To be able to draw a true representation of the scene in front of you, you need to look up at it, as well as down at your paper. What does the space around the object look like? Is that shadow grey, or is it actually blue? Does the apple you can see look like that, or are you drawing what you *think* an apple looks like?

Most children love to be creative; they are fearless about risking failure. So when does that stop? When did you tell yourself that you can't draw, or who was it that made you feel you couldn't?

Most importantly of all, if you think of your creation as art, then that's what it is, whether or not it is regarded as such by someone else. And that means everything can be art – from Jackson Pollock's drip paintings, hanging in the Tate Modern, to your toddler's latest creation, *Untitled*, stuck proudly on the fridge door.

❯ Arushi Bhatnagar, the world's youngest professional artist, had her first solo exhibition when she was 11 months old.

❯ The original title of Maurice Sendak's *Where the Wild Things Are* was *Where the Wild Horses Are*, until Sendak realised he couldn't draw horses.

❯ In Iceland, drawing a map on your letters and parcels can work just as well as an address.

❯ To 'screeve' is to draw on the pavement with coloured chalk.

❯ It was compulsory for 18th-century Prussian soldiers to have a beard. Those who couldn't grow one were told to draw one on.

Which polka came first, the dot or the dance?

The dance. It made everyone go dotty.

The polka was the dance craze of the 1840s – at least as big as the Charleston of the 1920s or the twist in the 1960s. As polkamania swept Britain and North America, manufacturers cashed in by adding the word 'polka' to products that were unconnected to the dance. You could buy polka hats and polka jackets, polka gauze, polka curtain ties and even polka ham. As far as we know, none of these had dots on them.

The first recorded mention of polka dots is from 1857, when manufacturers of spotted fabric decided to jump on the craze. Until then, spotted fabric was known as 'dotted Swiss'.

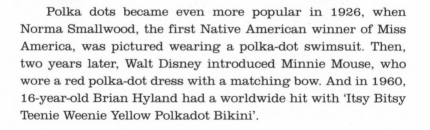

Polka dots became even more popular in 1926, when Norma Smallwood, the first Native American winner of Miss America, was pictured wearing a polka-dot swimsuit. Then, two years later, Walt Disney introduced Minnie Mouse, who wore a red polka-dot dress with a matching bow. And in 1960, 16-year-old Brian Hyland had a worldwide hit with 'Itsy Bitsy Teenie Weenie Yellow Polkadot Bikini'.

The polka is a Czech dance from Bohemia, which is to the south of Poland, but no one knows where the name comes from. It could be a portmanteau word (a shortened combination of two other words, like 'dancercise' from 'dance' + 'exercise'), using the names of two Polish dances – the polonaise and the mazurka. Or it could be from the Polish word *polka*, meaning 'a Polish woman'.

It's a Czech dance, though, so Czechs prefer the theory that it's from the Czech word *půlka*, 'half', after the little half-steps in the dance. But no one can say for sure.

We do know the origin of the word 'dot', though. It's from Old English *dott*, 'the head of a boil'.

······················ **DOTTY FACTS** ·····················

❯ Polka-Dot Man was an early enemy of Batman.

❯ Black Sabbath were originally called the Polka Tulk Blues Band.

❯ Until 2008, the Grammys had a Best Polka Album category. Of the 24 awarded over the years, Jimmy Sturr won 18.

The beginning of Beethoven's Fifth Symphony is the same as Morse code for 'V', and V is the Roman numeral for 5. Is it a coincidence?

The Fifth Symphony begins with the famous da-da-da-DUMMMM. And the Morse code for 'V' is 'dot dot dot dash', but, remarkably, there is no connection between the two.

Samuel Morse's system didn't actually contain any letters, only numbers. It was his colleague Alfred Vail who thought of adding letters to it. There is no evidence that Vail had Beethoven in mind when deciding on the code for the letter 'V'; rather, the letters were assigned dots and dashes depending on how frequently they were used – common letters had simple codes and rarer letters had longer ones. So 'E', the most common letter, is just 'dot', while 'X' is 'dash dot dash dash'. And 'V' became 'dot dot dot dash'.

Nobody appears to have connected the 'V' of Morse code and Beethoven's 5th (or Vth) until the Second World War. In January 1941, Belgian radio announcer Victor de Laveleye wanted a symbol of resistance to the Nazis and chose the letter 'V' because it was shared between the English word 'victory', the French equivalent, *victoire*, and the Flemish word *vrijheid*, meaning 'freedom'. Soon, the Belgian Resistance began drawing it everywhere. Then Douglas Ritchie, one of the BBC's wartime broadcasters, started broadcasting under the name 'Colonel Britton' to educate people about the symbol, encouraging people to make the 'V' sign at each other (and the Nazis). The genius who first made the connection between

'V' for Victory, the 'V' of Morse code and Beethoven's Fifth is unknown, but the BBC began playing the start of Beethoven's Fifth before its wartime broadcasts, telling people it stood for 'Victory'.

The Nazi government, infuriated by the constant 'V' signs, and especially annoyed that the German Beethoven was being pressed into service for the Allies, tried copying the idea and put up official German 'V' signs all over Europe. They hung huge 'V' banners off the Eiffel Tower and Amsterdam's royal palace, but the damage was already done – helped especially by Churchill sticking two fingers up whenever there was a camera about.

. . . .

How was Beethoven's Fifth Symphony first received?

The premiere of Beethoven's Fifth was not a huge success. The show lasted for four hours in a freezing theatre, one of the lead sopranos got stage fright, the Fifth and Sixth Symphonies were mislabelled in the programme, Beethoven had just had a huge row with the whole orchestra, and one reviewer said the orchestra's execution 'could be considered lacking in all respects'.

. . . . V. INTERESTING . . . .

❯ Beethoven started going deaf at 26. Some people think this was due to his habit of immersing his head in cold water to keep himself awake.

Why is pop music not as good as it used to be?

Music is becoming more generic. A 2012 study analysed 464,411 songs recorded between 1955 and 2010 and found that the most recent ones had less variation in pitch and volume. It also looked at 'timbral variety' (the difference between two notes of the same pitch and volume – because they're made by different instruments, for instance), observing that this peaked in the 1960s and has been declining ever since.

Moreover, many of the world's most popular pop songs are written by a select group of people. For example, since 1999, songwriter Max Martin has been credited on 23 US number one singles, for nine different artists, including Britney Spears, Taylor Swift and Maroon 5.

But there's also the matter of perception. As we age, we tend to have less time to listen to new songs, and by the age of 33 most people have stopped listening to new music altogether. A survey by the music streaming site Deezer found that 60% of its users simply listened to the same songs over and over. A psychological theory called the 'mere exposure effect' says that you prefer things if you're exposed to them more: you're not going to like new music if you don't listen to it.

There's also something called the 'reminiscence bump'. This is the idea that we tend to remember our young adult life as being our best years. Any music that you listened to when you were in your late teens and early 20s will be more ingrained in your psyche. That is, unless you get out there and listen to something new.

'We don't have Coke, is Pepsi okay?'

In 2004, American neuroscientist Samuel McClure and his team wired people up to a brain scanner and gave them both brands of cola, without revealing which was which. They found that the pleasure centres in the brain were more likely to light up when subjects were given Pepsi. However, when the participants were told what they were drinking, the brain scans showed the opposite.

It turns out that how much we like a drink depends on a combination of what it actually tastes like and what prior information we have about the brand. And that a lot of people who say they favour Coke actually prefer the taste of Pepsi. For those people, accepting a glass of Pepsi in the pub will be fine, but it would have been better if the bartender had never asked, 'Is Pepsi okay?' in the first place.

······················· FIZZY FACTS ······················

❭ In the 1940s, a Russian general secretly asked the US to create a clear version of Coca-Cola so he could pretend it was vodka and not a symbol of capitalist America.

❭ Pepsi was originally called Brad's Drink.

❭ Billionaire business tycoon Warren Buffett has at least five cans of Coca-Cola a day. In 2015, he stated he was 'one-quarter Coca-Cola'.

Is there really a worm called a 'bookworm'?

The word 'bookworm' was first used in the 1590s, when it had the same meaning as it does today: someone who likes to read. It wasn't used to describe the bugs that eat books until 1713.

Confusingly, while there are several types of insects who feed on books, none of them are worms. You can identify which pest is responsible by looking at how your book is damaged. If you can see holes in the page, they are probably the work of young beetles who tunnel into the pages for protection and dine on the starchy paper. If the book is also mouldy, it's probably psocids, or 'booklice', which eat microscopic mould. Silverfish (insects that get their name from their shimmering appearance and don't live in the sea) devour the nutritious organic ink in old books; this means the words might start to disappear before you've had a chance to read them.

If you are being bothered by bookworms (of any variety), the best treatment is to sprinkle your books with pepper, which repels them. Just be aware of any human bookworms looking for their next read, as it's bad manners to sneeze too loudly in a library.

· · · · · · · · · · · · · · · · · · · NOVEL FACTS · · · · · · · · · · · · · · · · · · ·

> There are 20 new books published in the UK every hour.

> In the 18th century, so many books went missing from Marsh's Library in Dublin that they ended up locking people in cages while they read.

> In 2018, a librarian in Hong Kong was arrested for falsely reporting library cards as missing so that borrowers would have to return books that she wanted to read.

What happens if you try to use superglue on a non-stick pan?

The ancient Greeks had non-stick pans. They made ceramics with dozens of tiny holes, which archaeologists believe would let the oil spread evenly and stop bread sticking as it cooked. Today's non-stick frying pans are covered in a chemical called polytetrafluoroethylene (PTFE for short). This is also known as Teflon, and it repels pretty much anything – including superglue. If the glue is put on a Teflon pan, it will turn into beads that can be easily washed off.

PTFE was invented by US chemist Roy Plunkett in 1938, but rather than looking for a material to help cook food, he was trying to create a new chemical to refrigerate it. Before it found its way into the kitchen, it was used in the manufacture of atomic bombs, making seals that could withstand the corrosive uranium gas.

Superglue was discovered in 1942 by scientists who were trying to make plastics for gun sights during the Second World War. It was originally thought to be useless because it was so sticky. It would be another 16 years before anyone realised the commercial applications and it appeared on our shelves.

So superglue was invented by accident while trying to create materiel for the war, and Teflon was used in the war

despite having been invented by accident for something else. The war between the two is – for the moment – being won by the non-stick pan.

Do they deliberately sweeten the delicious glue on the back of envelopes?

The sap of the acacia tree is known as gum arabic. When the trees are wounded, they use this substance to seal the splits in their own bark, a process called 'gummosis'. But it also makes the perfect glue for envelopes, because it becomes sticky when exposed to moisture. It has a slightly sweet taste, but that's just a lucky coincidence.

Gum arabic is also used in watercolour paint, shoe polish and newspaper ink. And it is used by soft-drinks manufacturers to stop all the sugar from settling at the bottom of the can. Fortunately, the rest of the flavours in your fizzy drink manage to mask the slight taste of envelopes.

In the early 2000s, some American firms added spearmint or peppermint flavouring into their return envelopes as a little treat for customers. The trend petered out, and these days there is only one company in the US making flavoured stationery. Flavorlopes provide apple-, cherry-, grape- and (around Christmas time) eggnog-flavoured envelopes.

······························ POST-TRUTH ·····························

❯ Self-adhesive stamps were first sold to the British public in 1993, but the first country to make them was Sierra Leone, way back in 1964: they came in very useful in a country that was so humid that traditional stamps didn't work all that well.

Why does cooking ham make lots of holes in the tin foil?

The effect is caused by sparks of electricity jumping from the foil onto the food. In fact, you've essentially made a mini-lightning storm in your kitchen.

Aluminium is a very reactive substance; it's desperate to interact with its surroundings. Even though it's the most common metal on Earth, it's never found on its own in nature because it always bonds with another material. In your oven, if you cook foil-covered food in a steel pan, the aluminium in the foil will try to bond with the cookware. To do this, it has to share electrons (tiny negative particles) with the pan. Wherever food touches the foil, the moisture on its surface acts as the electrons' mode of transport to carry them between foil and pan. Electrons like travelling across salty substances, such as cured meat, which is why ham is particularly susceptible. They also love acidic liquids, like any tomato-based sauce. That's why this effect is sometimes known as a 'lasagne battery'.

When electrons jump from one place to another, they make electricity and often leave a path of destruction. This might come in the form of a felled tree, when they travel as lightning, or the result might be small holes in tin foil. But rest assured that while you might notice specks of dark residue on your food, it is still good to eat. These fragments are the remnants of disintegrated aluminium, but there isn't enough to do you any damage or affect the taste. Bon appétit!

Can humans eat grass?

Grass isn't poisonous, so theoretically you could eat it without suffering serious side effects, but it won't do you any good, and you don't know where it's been. Or rather, you do know where it's been, but you don't know who's been on it.

Grass does contain some nutritional value, in the form of carbohydrates and protein, but they're trapped within a tough material called cellulose, which our stomachs can't break down. This means that if you swallow a blade of grass, it will come out of the other end almost entirely unchanged.

Cows get past this problem with the help of the millions of bacteria that live in their stomachs. These consume the outer casing of the grass, releasing the remaining nutrients for the cow to enjoy. If we could somehow get these bacteria into our digestive tracts, perhaps through a specially made probiotic yoghurt, we too would be able to add grass to our menus.

The bacteria in cows' stomachs need plenty of time to break through the cellulose, which is why cows take up to three days to digest one meal and their intestines are about 20 times their body length. Humans' intestines are, by contrast, only three to four times as long as our bodies – roughly the same proportion as in elephants.

. . . . TODAY I LAWNED . . . .

❯ The grass on the tennis courts at Wimbledon is cut to a height of exactly 8 mm during the championships.

❯ *Math* is an Old English word for 'a mowing of grass'. An 'aftermath' was the second mowing, which took place after the first harvest.

Why am I a capital letter, when you are not?

English is the only language that capitalises the first-person pronoun 'I'. Even in German, which capitalises every noun, from *Prinzessin* (princess) to *Pampelmuse* (grapefruit), as well as the more formal version of the word for 'you' (*Sie*), the word for 'I', *ich*, is written in humble lower case. Danish does capitalise the word *I*, but it means 'you', and the reason for this capitalisation is the same as in English: in both countries it was decided that if a single letter was going to serve such an important purpose, it should be enlarged.

In Old English the word for 'I' was *ich* (pronounced like 'itch') or *ic*, but in the 1200s people in the north of England started dropping the ending and just saying 'i'. The habit spread to the south, and influential writers, such as Chaucer in his *Canterbury Tales*, capitalised it, probably encouraged by the fact that a lone, stranded 'i' made it look like a writer's finger had slipped or a letter had gone missing.

The words *ich*, 'i' and 'I' coexisted for a few centuries before 'I' became universal, because spelling and grammar rules were looser in the past. For instance, Shakespeare used the phrase 'between you and I' in his writing, instead of 'between you and me'. Linguists today have labelled this habit 'a grammatical error of unsurpassable grossness'. However, between You and *ich*, it probably doesn't matter quite as much as they think.

Have I read this page before?

The first person to give an explanation for déjà vu – the spooky feeling that something seems oddly familiar – was St Augustine of Hippo. Augustine is the patron saint of brewers, because he lived a life of debauchery and partying before giving it all up to become a monk. He thought déjà vu was caused by 'deceitful spirits' who were trying to sow confusion. Perhaps this was because, for him, any flashbacks might be related to his sinful past.

The phrase 'déjà vu', which translates as 'already seen', was coined by the 19th-century French philosopher Émile Boirac, who was the president of Dijon University but spent most of his time doing experiments on clairvoyance and mysticism. He believed déjà vu was due to emotions, and thought that if you have the same emotional feelings in two different situations then your mind might accidentally confuse the two.

Déjà vu is still a bit of a mystery, but the current best theory is that it's your brain doing a quick memory stock-check. When you're in a situation that is similar to one you've experienced in the past, your brain gets confused and sends signals of familiarity, along with a feeling of slight unease. Researchers say that it's a good sign, indicating that your faculties are in full working order, which could explain why it's more common in younger people, who tend to have a better memory.

Perhaps you're revisiting this page in the full knowledge that you've read it before. Studies show that people often enjoy watching TV shows, films and books more, or in a different way, the second time around. But you knew that already.

Does anyone have a photographic memory?

Nobody can see a page of type, blink and recall it with perfect accuracy whenever they like. But there are some people who get pretty close.

A fraction of adults – fewer than a hundred in the whole world – have a condition called Highly Superior Autobiographical Memory (HSAM). They can tell you, for example, what they had for lunch on a particular day 20 years ago. One person with HSAM is Bob Petrella, who remembers up to half the days of his entire life in detail, and most of his conversations for the last 63 years. When he lost his phone in 2006, he didn't worry: all the numbers were in his head.

In 1970, Harvard scientist Charles Stromeyer III published a scientific paper about a student called Elizabeth, who appeared to have a genuinely 'photographic' memory. She could memorise patterns consisting of tens of thousands of random dots and keep them in her head for over a day. But then Charles and Elizabeth got married, and she refused to be tested again. No other such person has ever been found.

The nearest thing to 'photographic' memory is something called 'eidetic' memory. Up to 15% of children have it, but almost no adults. If someone with eidetic memory is shown an image, they can 'see' a vivid after-image for several minutes, almost like a snapshot, which they can describe. The downside is that it doesn't work with anything as complex as a page of text, and it's never perfect.

There are also trained memorisers. Ben Pridmore from Derby was world memory champion several times. He could recall the order of a shuffled pack of cards in 24 seconds, using a technique called a 'memory palace'. It works like this. You hold a vivid image in your mind's eye of somewhere you know really well (like a room or a street). You pass through it, visualising each item you want to remember in a specific part of the location, thereby associating the two.

It's a skill with limits, though. Interviewed in 2007, Pridmore couldn't remember where he'd set his world memory record, or which memory records he held. He also cheerfully admitted he frequently went into a room and forgot what he'd gone in for.

· **MEMORABLE FACTS** ·

❯ The current record for memorising a deck of cards is 13.96 seconds, held by China's Zou Lujian.

❯ Just imagining walking through a door can make you forget what you were thinking.

❯ Heading a football can give you memory problems for up to 24 hours.

❯ Dolphins can remember each other after 20 years apart.

Why do Olympic racers run anticlockwise?

Some people think races are anticlockwise due to biology. Most people are 'righties', meaning that their right hands and legs are dominant, and running in an anticlockwise direction means that their right leg is doing a bit more work. Others have suggested that anticlockwise races are preferred because it's better for the spectators, rather than the racers. When runners are going anticlockwise, they move from left to right in front of the crowd, which is what seems like the 'correct' direction of travel for most people. It is, after all, how you're reading the words in this book.

Throughout history, however, there have been plenty of clockwise races, which does appear to undermine the idea that there is some sort of natural direction of travel. In the first few modern Olympic Games, from 1896 to 1906, all the races were clockwise, and the athletics societies at Oxford and Cambridge University were running clockwise races into the 1940s and 1950s.

The ancient Greeks didn't have to worry about which way to run. In the early Olympics, runners went in a straight line down a length of track called a *stadion*, which was about 180 metres in length. For longer races, runners would just turn around and run back.

So it seems that there's no definitive answer for why races are now run in an anticlockwise direction, and trying to pin one down just sends us round in circles.

What were the terms for 'clockwise' and 'anticlockwise' before clocks were invented?

5,000 years before mechanical clocks were invented, the ancient Egyptians and Babylonians used sundials to track the Sun's shadow throughout the day. As the hours passed, the shadow moved in the same direction as the hands of clocks do today, and so people always referred to the Sun when describing a clockwise motion.

'Sunwise' was one old term for 'clockwise'; 'sungates' was another. The opposite was 'withershins' (or 'widdershins'), which meant going the wrong way or in the opposite direction to the Sun. Because it was against the usual order of things, it was seen as unlucky or sinister. If you talk about giving someone a 'withering' look, you're using a related word.

However, this is true only in the northern hemisphere. The Sun moves anticlockwise south of the equator, so if modern clock faces had evolved from sundials in Australia, for instance, the hands would all move in the opposite direction.

What do 'a.m.' and 'p.m.' mean?

They both come from Latin. The abbreviation 'a.m.' stands for *ante meridiem*, or 'before midday', while 'p.m.' is short for *post meridiem*, or 'after midday'.

················ A SECOND-HAND FACT ····················

❯ Clocks didn't have second or minute hands until the 1600s.

Why do the numbers on a telephone keypad go the opposite way to the ones on a calculator?

Everybody knows Alexander Graham Bell invented the telephone. Except he didn't. Italian inventor Antonio Meucci had already had the idea and a patent. Unfortunately, it lapsed when he couldn't afford the renewal fee, so when Bell submitted his own design in 1876, he received the full credit.

Among his accolades, Bell was awarded a prize of 50,000 francs by the French government, which he used to set up a laboratory. One of his employees there was a South African psychologist named John E. Karlin, whose job was to make the telephones as efficient and easy to use as possible.

One of Karlin's projects concerned the length of a telephone handset cord. They were made with copper, which was in short supply after the war, and so the shorter they could be made, the better. Karlin snuck into his colleagues' offices and shortened the cords on their phones by a small amount each day. They didn't notice until he had taken an entire foot, so that's the amount they decided to remove.

In 1950s America, each local area was served by a 'hub' with a two-letter code that people had to dial to get through to that neighbourhood. This is why phone numbers in old films sometimes start with letters. Karlin thought this system was outdated, so he invented the idea of area codes, and everyone's phone numbers suddenly became much longer. Telephones at the time used a rotary dial to place a call, and Karlin realised buttons would be better – but no one knew how to arrange them.

Bell's lab already had a design where the buttons were spread over two rows. Karlin trialled this, along with options where the buttons were displayed in a circle (to mimic the rotary phones) and in a rectangle, with 1, 2 and 3 either at the bottom (as in a calculator) or at the top (the design that we see today). The results were clear. People much preferred the rectangular system, and having 1, 2 and 3 at the top resulted in fewer mistakes. The * and # keys were added later, to make a 12-key grid.

One day, at a cocktail party, Karlin was recognised as the inventor of the area code by a fellow partygoer. He was thrilled to be spotted, until she asked: 'How does it feel to be the most hated man in America?' Something tells us that they didn't end up swapping numbers.

What number is the answer to life, the universe and everything?

Most people would say 42. In ancient Egyptian mythology, you are asked 42 questions as you travel through the afterlife, and it's the number of laws in the game of cricket. And, of course, in the book *The Hitchhiker's Guide to the Galaxy* it's the answer given to the question 'What is the answer to life, the universe and everything?' But, for scientists, another number keeps cropping up.

That number is 0.007297351 – not quite as catchy as 42, although you could write it as $\frac{1}{137}$. Physicists call it the 'fine structure constant', and it is represented by the Greek letter α. 0.007297351 is a number that keeps appearing when you combine three of the most important concepts of the universe: the speed of light in a vacuum, the electrical charge of one electron and Planck's constant (the 'quantum' in quantum mechanics – or, if you want to be technical, the ratio of a photon of light's energy to its frequency). It doesn't matter if they're measured in miles, kilometres, joules, coulombs or the length of a double-decker bus – the number keeps appearing. And it's led a lot of scientists to wonder if it is pointing to something important that they can't yet understand.

Some physicists say we should project the number into space to let other cultures know that we're an intelligent life form with an understanding of the universe. But others warn that we shouldn't tell aliens where we live in case that invites them to attack. If that's the case, we might be better scaring them off by sending them the rules of cricket.

Why is Friday the 13th so unlucky?

Today, everybody loves a Friday, but Jesus was crucified on (Good) Friday, so in medieval times it was associated with sadness. Similarly, the number 13 was seen as unlucky because Judas was the 13th person at the Last Supper, just before he betrayed Jesus.

In the 19th century, these two superstitions combined and Friday the 13th was marked as an unlucky date. Fear spread further in 1907, when an American businessman wrote a book called *Friday the 13th*, about a stock market crash that happened on that date. If you're keen to avoid it, then you can get a two-week head start by watching out for months that begin on a Sunday – they always have a Friday the 13th.

········· **TGIF (THANK GOODNESS IT'S FACTS)** ·············

❯ Fear of the number 13 is called 'triskaidekaphobia'.

❯ President Franklin D. Roosevelt refused to travel on Friday the 13th.

❯ Friday the 17th is feared in Italy, while in Spain it's Tuesday the 13th.

Where does money come from?

Money is any item that people have agreed is worth a certain amount. And it doesn't have to be coins or notes. Early humans used shells; medieval Europeans, squirrel pelts. On Yap Island in the Pacific, the currency was limestone discs up to 12ft tall, and the Aztecs used cacao beans. But any system is open to abuse. Aztec forgers emptied cacao pods and filled them with mud before passing them off as the real thing.

12 feet

2,500 years ago, the ancient Lydians of what is now Turkey invented metal coinage. What made their currency different was that the government backed the coins and guaranteed their value. 400 years later, the first banknotes appeared in China. They were made of deerskin and each was a foot wide. Paper notes were also invented in China, but it took another 700 years for them to replace the deerskins and for wallets to breathe a huge sigh of relief.

As for the money in your wallet today, the UK's banknotes are printed in Essex by De La Rue, the largest such manufacturer in the world. De La Rue has designed over a third of the world's banknotes and works with 140 different countries. The business has been struggling recently, though: it used to print all British passports as well, but the government chose to get the new, non-EU passports designed in France and made in Poland.

British coins, meanwhile, are made at the Royal Mint. Once housed at the Tower of London, it relocated in the 1960s to South Wales. To make a coin, molten metal is poured from a furnace into a mould and flattened into a continuous strip of the correct thickness. The coins are then punched out in the same way you'd cut circles out of pastry, at a rate of 10,000 discs – or 'blanks' – per minute. An imprint of the Queen's face is then stamped onto each blank with a force of 60 tonnes, a different image is added on the reverse, and the coin is ready to go into circulation.

You can't spend it at the Royal Mint itself, though. It's a cashless workplace.

· **BANK NOTES** ·

❯ In 2015, almost 70,000 people signed a petition urging the Australian government to change the name of the national currency to dollarydoos.

❯ Early American money was inscribed with the phrase 'To Counterfeit is Death'.

Why is a leap year so called?
What is being leapt over?

The day of the week that you have your birthday on usually moves forward by one day each year. However, leap years have an extra day on 29 February, which means the following 365 days move forward two places. For example, in 2017, 1 May was on a Monday, in 2018 on a Tuesday and in 2019 on a Wednesday. But in 2020, which was a leap year, 1 May was on a Friday. Thursday had been 'leapt' over.

Leap years are necessary because the Earth doesn't take exactly 365 days to go around the Sun; it takes 365 days, 5 hours, 48 minutes and 46 seconds. Left uncorrected, that extra quarter of a day builds up over the years, gradually nudging calendars out of sync with the Earth's orbit, and before you know it, it could be winter in June (or winter in December, if you're reading this in the southern hemisphere). Historically, this has caused a lot of problems, such as in 46 BC, when the Roman calendar was so at odds with our planet's movements that Julius Caesar decreed a single 445-day-long year to fix it. This was known as 'the last year of confusion'.

Our current calendar adds one extra day every four years on 29 February, but it also drops three of these leap days every 400 years to make sure the calculation is as precise as possible. So there is no leap day on years that end in '00' but which aren't divisible by 400, meaning that while 1700, 1800 and 1900 were not leap years, the year 2000 was. And if you can get your head around all that, you can take the day off.

Why do digital watches always seem to gain time?

95% of watches sold today are digital, and they are controlled by quartz. Quartz is one of the most common minerals on the planet: also known as silicon dioxide, it is the main ingredient of sand. Quartz is useful to watchmakers because of a curious property it has: when you run an electric current through it, it vibrates backwards and forwards, 32,768 times a second. Each digital watch has a sliver of quartz as thin as a sheet of paper inside, and when the watch's battery runs a current through it, the quartz starts vibrating. A tiny microchip in the watch counts the pulses, and every time it tots up 32,768 tiny vibrations, it adds one second to the time on the display. Simple.

However, quartz is temperamental. At higher temperatures it vibrates more quickly, which means the watch counts seconds faster than it should, making the watch run fast by up to 30 seconds a month. Changes in air pressure can also alter the rate at which quartz vibrates.

The first-ever digital watch, the Hamilton Pulsar, was introduced in 1972, and was described as 'a solid state wrist computer programmed to tell time'. It was partly based on the futuristic clocks the makers had designed as props for the film *2001: A Space Odyssey*, and adverts stressed that you didn't need to wind it, it made no ticking sound (it was described as being as silent as space) and it was much more accurate than existing timepieces. Today, you can buy a digital watch and get change from a tenner, but the Pulsar cost $2,100 – at the time, more than a gold Rolex.

Why do men go bald – and always in the same way?

It'd be more fun if baldness came in a range of styles – cookie-cutter circles, or stripes, or starting from the back of the neck – but in the case of male-pattern baldness, at least, it's always the same. The hair on the top of the head departs from the centre outwards. And at the front, it's the reverse: the centre holds, while baldness creeps in from left and right, leaving an 'M'-shape on the forehead.

It all starts inside the testes, where most of the male sex hormone testosterone is made. It's what gives men their deep voices, their beards and their sex drives. And it's also what takes away their hair.

Or, at least, redistributes it. Hairs around the body respond to testosterone in different ways, meaning that as men's hair starts going thin on top, their backs and ears start sprouting. Testosterone shrivels up the follicles (from the Latin for 'little bags') in the scalp, squeezing out each resident hair. Women produce much less of this hair-thinning hormone, and so are less likely to go bald. Testosterone giveth and testosterone taketh away. And no one knows why.

Baldness seems to spread from one hair to the next, like a virus. If you take a working follicle next to a bald patch and transplant it to somewhere hairier – the crotch, say – the hair will still drop out, as if in long-distance touch with its former neighbour. Conversely, if you take follicles from a hairy part of the body and transplant them to a bald bit, they will flourish as before. This is how hair transplants work.

Another thing we don't know is why baldness always

follows the same template. The latest (not very convincing) idea is that gravity is responsible. At the very top of your head, so the theory goes, the weight of the whole rest of the scalp is pulling on the follicles, which is why men get a bald spot there first. At the front, it's the weight of your face pulling at the follicles on the top of your forehead and temples – the bit at the side of your head stays hairy because your ears are holding the follicles up. Oh, come on. Pull the other one, scientists. The best thing a man can do with baldness is accept it. Take Bruce Willis as a role model and just tell people you have too much testosterone.

······················ **BALD-FACED TRUTHS** ·····················

❯ Baldness was the reason Julius Caesar wore a laurel wreath.

❯ Ancient Egyptians applied lotions made of boiled porcupine quills or a female greyhound's leg fried in oil with a donkey's hoof.

❯ The Vikings tried to stop baldness by rubbing goose faeces into the scalp.

❯ More short men go bald than tall men.

Why do we sneeze? And why do some people sneeze more loudly than others?

Sneezing is your body's way of removing something unwanted from your nose. If the hairs inside your nostrils sense something unusual, they send a message to your brain that causes your muscles to spasm, air to rush from your lungs and mucus to fly out of your mouth and nose.

But it doesn't always work first time, so sometimes your body needs to sneeze again, and sometimes even for a third or fourth time. Some people say that if you sneeze 10 times in a row, you will die. That's obviously not true, but it could be a sign that you have limited lung capacity and that your body can't get enough air to pass through your nose and dislodge the irritation. (There is a persistent playground rumour that if you burp, fart and sneeze at the same time, you will die – again, fortunately, untrue.)

The noise you make when sneezing seems to be largely pointless. The air rushing through your nose makes a sound, of course, but there's no logical reason for you to say 'achoo'. In fact, the sound you produce when sneezing is entirely cultural: it's 'hatschi' in German, 'hakshon' in Japanese and 'Apch-hee' in Hebrew. And deaf people tend to sneeze without saying any word at all.

If I sneeze with my eyes open, will my eyeballs pop out?

This is one of the few playground rumours with a tiny kernel of truth to it. When you sneeze, your eyes close to protect them from what's coming out of your nose, not to stop them from popping out, but it has been known for the force of a sneeze to cause a dislocation of the eyeball. It can happen only if you have an underlying problem with the muscles around your eyes or if you suffer from 'floppy eyelid syndrome'. Mercifully, both of these issues are extremely rare.

Why don't we sneeze in our sleep?

Some of the things that make you sneeze when you're awake simply aren't an issue when you're asleep. People sneeze when they see bright lights – not a problem at night-time; others sneeze after disturbing something dusty – also unlikely at night, unless you are sleepwalking.

On top of that, your body has mechanisms to stop you snoozing and sneezing at the same time. When you dream, you enter REM (rapid eye movement) sleep, which allows your eyes to move around, but your other muscles are temporarily paralysed. This prevents you from hurting yourself, but it also means that the signals that would usually tell your body to prepare to sneeze don't get sent.

If there's a big enough irritant (like someone putting a feather up your nose), then you might sneeze, but even then you'll wake up moments before you do so.

Why don't people's eyebrows grow as long as the hair on their head?

The longest eyebrow hair ever recorded belonged to a man called Zheng Shusen from China. Even though it was 7.5 inches long and kept getting in his mouth, he saw it as a blessing. In 2016, when applying for a Guinness World Record, he wrote that in China, long eyebrows are a symbol of long life. Whenever the hair got really troublesome, Shusen would tuck it behind his ear.

The longest ear hair on record is a touch shorter, at 7.1 inches, while the longest nipple hair is 6.7 inches. But impressive as all these records are, they are dwarfed by the longest hair on a human head, which belonged to Xie Qiuping from China and stretched for 18 feet.

Your head hair and your eyebrow hair are there for different reasons. Head hair keeps your head from getting cold; eyebrow hair is there to keep sweat out of your eyes. While having more hair up top keeps you warmer, if your eyebrows got too long, they'd poke into your eyes (or, worse still, your mouth). So each hair follicle has a gene that acts like a switch, telling it when to stop growing. In head-hair follicles the switch flips off after a few years, while in your eyebrows it takes only a few months. Sometimes these genes send the wrong message, which is why you might find a rogue long hair somewhere it's not supposed to be.

How did people trim their nails before nail clippers were invented?

The first nail-clipper patents were registered in the late 19th century by Valentine Fogarty in the US and David Gestetner in the UK. However, Gestetner's circular nail-clipper wasn't his only contribution to the world of filing, as he also designed a precursor to the photocopier.

Prior to the mass production of nail-clippers, the polite way to trim your nails was with a small knife. In 20 BC, the ancient Roman poet Horace wrote about the practice: 'A close-shaven man, it's said, in an empty barber's booth, penknife in hand, quietly cleaning his nails.' There's also a reference to nail-trimming in the Old Testament.

Many of those who didn't have access to a barber or penknife would have short nails anyway, thanks to a life of manual labour, and failing that there was always nature's nail-clippers – their teeth.

·················· **QUICK CLIPPINGS** ··················

❯ In Norse mythology there was a mythical ship called *Naglfar*, made from the toenails and fingernails of the dead.

❯ There is a Japanese superstition that if you cut your nails at night, then terrible things will happen to your family.

If horses get sore feet from not having their hooves taken care of by farriers, how did they cope before humans?

A horse's hoof is actually a very large, strong middle finger (or toe), with an outer layer that is mostly keratin, like an enormous fingernail. And just like your fingernails, the horse's keratin layer is always growing, meaning domesticated horses need frequent trims so that they can walk in comfort. Horses used to have five full toes on their feet, back when they were the size of dogs, but as they evolved, they grew bigger, and walking on a single big toe was more efficient and stress-free than walking on several smaller ones

In the wild, horses spend their days walking long distances over uneven and rough grassland, which makes their hooves harder and stronger over time, as well as naturally trimming them down to the right length. Domesticated horses need a lot more hoof care because they spend so much of their time standing around in stables and paddocks. Not only do they get less exercise, but any they do receive is often over softer or damper ground, which means their hooves need much more frequent manicuring.

· **STABLE GENIUS** ·

❯ The Romans used removable horseshoes known as 'hipposandals'.

❯ The ancient Greeks enjoyed eating donkeys' feet.

If you have heartburn when you are pregnant, will you have a hairy baby?

You actually might . . . The idea that a hairy baby gives its mother heartburn from inside the womb dates back at least 150 years. But nobody tested the idea until 2006, when scientists at America's Johns Hopkins University decided to look into it. And, amazingly, they found out that it's true.

The researchers took notes on 64 pregnant women throughout their pregnancy and recorded whether or not they suffered heartburn. Then, after the subjects had given birth, two impartial observers looked at the resulting babies and rated how hairy they were. Of the 28 women who reported moderate to strong heartburn, 23 had babies with either average or above average amounts of hair on their heads. Conversely, almost all the women who reported zero heartburn were likely to have babies with very little hair.

Heartburn has nothing to do with the heart; it's caused by acid travelling out of the stomach and up into the throat. Usually, there's a ring of muscle at the bottom of your oesophagus which stops the acid, but high levels of oestrogen can cause that muscle to relax. It turns out that this same hormone also influences hair growth in foetuses – so the same chemicals are behind both heartburn and hair.

Why is loss of memory linked to having a baby, and does it ever come back?

Expectant mothers call it 'baby brain', 'preg head' or 'mumnesia', but scientists have only recently confirmed that it actually exists. Specifically, studies have found that women perform less well on unfamiliar memory tasks when pregnant. For instance, they'd have little trouble recalling the words to a song they'd heard multiple times but would struggle more than usual to remember new lyrics. The change isn't drastic; researchers stress that these women's abilities remain within the normal range, 'albeit at the lower end'. More reassuringly, memory returns to its full pre-pregnancy level within a couple of years of giving birth. The fact that it takes this long is unsurprising when you consider the sleeplessness, multitasking and increased stress levels associated with looking after a baby.

While the memory loss caused by pregnancy is only temporary, the changes to the brain itself can be permanent. After giving birth, the parts of a mother's brain responsible for empathy and social skills change size and shape. This may explain why the initial memory loss happens: the brain is spending less energy remembering song lyrics and phone numbers, and instead is building up the sections that handle emotional awareness, since these are more important for child-rearing. A baby will be more appreciative of a mother who understands why it's crying than one who can recite 100 digits of pi.

Why do humans have baby teeth?

Babies are born with all the teeth they'll ever have already in their heads, but none of them are visible in their mouths. Instead, they're squashed together inside the gums.

The first to 'erupt' into the mouth are the milk teeth, which act as smaller, substitute teeth for the first six to twelve years of our lives, because young children's mouths aren't big enough to accommodate the permanent ones. As the jaw grows, gaps appear between the baby teeth, making them less fit for purpose. At this point the larger, adult teeth step in, forcing the substitutes out as they emerge.

Do other animals have baby teeth?

Most mammals have two sets of teeth that work just like ours, though you probably haven't noticed it in your pets because they tend to swallow their baby teeth when they fall out. Rats and mice shed their milk teeth in the womb and are born with the second set already in place. Their teeth continue to grow at a rate of about five inches a year, which is why they have to gnaw on rough surfaces to wear them down.

Elephants, manatees and kangaroos are the exceptions. They use their front two teeth, but have more at the back of their mouths. When the front ones have worn down, they fall out and the pair behind them moves forward to replace them.

What can I do about garlic breath?

You're going to have to stop eating it or ask those around you to eat some as well.

Your brain is constantly phasing out unimportant sensations. This is called 'neural adaptation'. It's why your socks might feel quite tight on your feet when you first put them on, but you don't notice them for the rest of the day. Similarly, if you move from the countryside to the city, you might be irritated by the constant hum of traffic, but it won't be long before you forget it's there. It's also why if you smell of garlic, you get used to it, and the only sure-fire way your friends can be spared from the smell is if their brains start to phase it out as well.

One of the reasons garlic is so effective at making people smell is that the offensive-smelling molecules enter your bloodstream and travel round your whole body. This is why you can't get rid of the smell by brushing your teeth. It also means that you will still have garlic breath even if the garlic was inserted straight into your stomach via a tube. One doctor wrote a letter to the *Journal of the American Medical Association* about a woman who had eaten garlic shortly before birth and ended up with a garlicky baby.

If my skin rubs off all the time, why are tattoos permanent?

Your skin cells last only about two weeks before they are replaced, so if you write a phone number on the back of your hand and don't wash, you have a fortnight or so to make the call before it has totally faded away. Tattoos are different because it's not your skin cells that hold the ink, it's your white blood cells. When the tattoo artist's needle injects ink under your skin, your body thinks it's being attacked and specialised immune cells (large white blood cells known as macrophages) devour the ink and stop it from infecting any other part of your body. Once each macrophage is full, it stays where it is, holding the ink until the end of its life. When a macrophage eventually grows old, it releases the ink, which is immediately gobbled up by another macrophage, and the tattoo stays in place.

19% of adult Britons with a tattoo regret it, so there's a booming market in tattoo removal. Modern removal techniques involve lasers that break up the ink-filled macrophages, with different frequencies being used for different colours. Black and dark colours are very easy to remove, but greens and yellows take more time. Once the ink has been broken up, it enters the bloodstream and is then passed out of the body as urine, faeces or sweat.

· · · · · · · · · · · · · · · SOMETHING TO INK ABOUT · · · · · · · · · · · · · · · · ·

❯ Getting multiple tattoos can improve your immune system.

❯ The tattoo policy of the US Marine Corps is 32 pages long.

Why do bees die if they sting you, but wasps don't?

There are 20,000 different kinds of bees. Most of them don't die if they sting you, and some don't sting at all. Of the aggressive species, it's only the female bees that attack, and whether this is fatal to them or not depends on the shape of their stinger. Bees with straight stingers can sting as often as they like and be absolutely fine. Female worker honeybees, however, have ridged stingers that get caught in your skin, and the bee can't release itself without tearing its abdomen, which destroys its body beyond repair. This doesn't happen with all their stings, though: bees attack other insects much more often than humans, and since insects don't have such tough skin, the stinger comes straight out.

All female wasps have smooth stingers, which means that when they sting you, it slides out again and they can fly away. Sometimes this happens so quickly that you don't even see the culprit, only the mark they leave behind.

You might wonder why honeybees have evolved such a self-defeating defence strategy, but it is ultimately a means of protecting the queen (who has a straight stinger) and the rest of the hive. As the stinger can't be released, the bee injects the maximum amount of venom possible in an attempt to deter the threat. The bee also releases pheromones that alert other honeybees about your location in case one sting isn't enough.

The best way to protect yourself from a swarm of bees is to avoid disturbing them in the first place, but if you do catch their attention, your best move is to run and find an enclosed space, such as inside a car, to wait it out.

Which hurts more, a wasp sting or a bee sting?

A wasp's sting is more painful because their stinger penetrates deeper into the skin and they can sting you multiple times. What you really need to watch out for, though, are hornets – essentially, giant wasps with even larger stingers. They are known to defend their nests fiercely.

········· **UN-BEE-LIEVABLE** ···················

❯ When a honeybee stings, it begins to smell faintly of bananas.

❯ Bees that return to the hive drunk are not allowed in.

❯ The bumblebee used to be called the 'humblebee'.

❯ Queen bees were known as king bees until the 1600s, when they were found to have ovaries.

Why are some animals nocturnal?

It makes sense for humans to come out in the day and sleep at night: in the daytime there's warm sunshine and we can see what we're doing, whereas at night it can be cold and scary. However, for the first 200 million years of their existence, all mammals lived the night shift.

One reason for this is that sunshine and heat weren't helpful for fertility. If sperm is too warm, it is less effective. Males hadn't evolved scrotums at this point, and the testicles help to regulate the temperature of sperm. The Earth was warmer 200 million years ago, so the cool of the night helped to keep mammals fertile. In fact, even today humans are the exception to the rule, as most mammals are nocturnal. Thank goodness for external scrotums.

It was also safer to be nocturnal. It's thought that most dinosaurs were diurnal (active during the daytime), and so popping your head out of the burrow while the Sun was up could result in you becoming lunch for a passing T. rex. Some dinosaurs were active at night, but at least there were more dark corners for mammals to hide in.

Even though there are no dinosaurs left, it still makes sense for a lot of mammals to hide during the day. Rabbits are active during darkness because while the hawks that prey on them have great eyesight, it doesn't work as well in moonlight. Lions have better night vision than zebras, so they go on the prowl when the Sun goes down to improve their chances.

In the 1880s, mongooses were introduced to Hawaiian plantations to help control the rat population, but since rats are nocturnal and mongooses are diurnal, the two species never encountered each other. The farmers were stuck with double the number of critters to deal with, meaning they had to keep them away by working in the fields both day and night.

❯ To help them see in the dark, owls have such big eyes that they can't rotate them in their sockets at all.

❯ Although there are dozens of theories, Mozart may have died from too little sunlight: at the end of his life he was almost completely nocturnal.

❯ A rainbow created by moonlight is called a 'moonbow'.

❯ Wild hamsters can run up to 10 km a night.

Why do octopuses have blue blood and more than one heart?

Our blood is made up of red blood cells and plasma. The red blood cells transport oxygen around the body and contain haemoglobin, which is made of proteins and iron, and which gives our blood its red colour. The haemoglobin grabs on to the oxygen when blood passes through the lungs, travels downstream with it in the arteries and drops it off when it reaches its destination. Once the oxygen has been delivered, the blood returns back to the lungs via the veins to pick up more oxygen and repeat the minute-long loop.

Octopuses don't have haemoglobin in their blood. They have a substance called haemocyanin, which contains copper instead of iron, and this means it is blue rather than red. There are no red blood cells, so haemocyanin simply floats around in the plasma, like swimmers with no boat. Octopuses have haemocyanin rather than haemoglobin because it transfers oxygen much better in the cold waters of the ocean, but it's still not quite efficient enough to work without a bit of extra help. This help comes in the form of the octopus's three hearts: it has two to pump blood to its gills and help it breathe, while the other gets blood to the rest of its organs.

Can animals have blood of other colours?
Yes. Some marine worms, including the fat innkeeper worm, have purple blood. Sea cucumbers and beetles have yellow blood.

How do we know that no two snowflakes are the same?

Every snowflake starts with a speck of dust, dirt or pollen, around which tiny molecules of water attach themselves. On average, there are about 10^{19}, or ten billion billion, of these molecules in every single flake. Each one can attach to its neighbours in lots of different ways, some look slightly different to others and their general shape is influenced by temperature and humidity. If the temperature is 2°C, then you will have a flat hexagon. If it drops below that, you will suddenly have a big long needle. If it drops even lower, you get those star-shaped snowflakes with clover-like extensions on the end of their arms.

Because of how many molecules there are, and how the small differences add up, you would need about $10^{10,000,000,000,000,000,000}$ (10 followed by 10,000,000,000,000,000,000 zeros) Earths to have a chance of producing just one pair of identical snowflakes. We have only one Earth, so we can say with a reasonable amount of confidence that on a molecular level, no two snowflakes have ever been identical.

·················· SNOWLEDGE ··························

❯ In 1555, the Swedish scholar Olaus Magnus became the first European to depict snowflakes. According to him, the wide variety of shapes includes an arrow, a bell and a human hand.

Why are all planets round?

Our universe has at least one sextillion planets. A sextillion is a number so huge, it's virtually impossible to imagine, but to put it into some kind of context, the Earth weighs about a sextillion times more than a polar bear. It's a big number. But every single one of the sextillion planets in the universe is round. There isn't a single cuboid, dodecahedral or Toblerone-shaped one among them.

A planet begins as a cloud of rocks and dust particles rotating around a star. The particles attract each other due to gravity, until they form a single blob. As that blob attracts more matter, it gets bigger and bigger, until it has collected everything in its path. Since gravity works in all directions equally, the blob becomes round. Imagine a crowd of a thousand people all trying to get as close as possible to a circular bar in a pub. If the queue was six deep on one side of the bar and two deep on the other, then new arrivals would join the shorter queue and eventually the queues would even out, leaving a circular throng of thirsty punters. That's how gravity works in this case.

The roundness is not perfect, though. The Earth, for example, is an 'oblate spheroid': it's nearly spherical but has a bulge at the middle. This is because of the planet's spin. Every time the Earth rotates once on its axis, the middle travels further than the top. This means that land at the equator is moving faster than land at the poles, and the faster something spins, the more it is thrown outwards. Just like the rest of us, once it reaches a certain age, a new planet always gets a bulge around its middle.

The Earth's spare tyre is not very big: a hole through the planet would be only about 27 miles longer if it started at the equator than if it was pole to pole. The effect is much bigger on other planets that are not quite so solid. Saturn, which is largely made of gas, has a diameter that is 7,000 miles longer between two points on its equator than between its poles. This extra thickness can yield dramatic results too: if a planet gathers enough extra mass around its middle, the whole lot can be flung into space, eventually forming into a moon. But if you're hoping for a cube-shaped moon, you'll be waiting for quite a while.

Are all moons round?

Asteroids and moons are smaller than planets, so they have less gravity, and this means they're less round. Comet 67P is a trillionth of the weight of Earth (it weighs about the same as a billion polar bears) and is shaped like a very odd rubber duck.

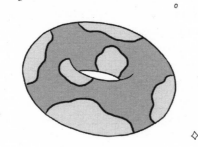

······················ **OUT-OF-THIS-WORLD FACTS** ·····················

❯ Stars can steal planets from each other as they pass by.

❯ Jupiter's moon Ganymede and Saturn's moon Titan are both larger than the planet Mercury.

❯ Ploonets are moons that have come free from the orbit of their planet and taken up a new orbit around a star. Scientists haven't found any yet, but they believe they may be out there.

Why isn't Pluto a planet any more?

In the early 1900s, US astronomer Percival Lowell noticed that the orbits of Neptune and Uranus were a bit unusual: there appeared to be a strange force acting on them that he couldn't explain. Lowell thought it was probably the effect of gravity from an undiscovered planet, and he made it his mission to find this mysterious object, which he called 'Planet X'.

Working from his observatory, the astronomer devoted the last years of his life to searching for a world beyond Neptune, but he died in 1916 without finding definitive evidence. Then, 14 years later, Clyde Tombaugh, a young assistant at Lowell's still-operative observatory, proved Lowell's prediction right, photographing the object that would become the ninth planet.

Tombaugh and the observatory team received more than 1,000 suggestions from the public as to what they should call the new body. Venetia Burney, an 11-year-old schoolgirl from Oxford, suggested Pluto, after the Roman god of the underworld, and the name was chosen, partly because the first two letters are 'P' and 'L', the initials of Percival Lowell. Venetia received £5 as a reward.

In the early 1990s, Pluto's status came into question. Lots of other objects were being discovered that were similar in size and mass. If Pluto was a planet, why weren't they?

In 2006, the International Astronomical Union settled the matter by strictly defining what a planet is. They said that all planets had to:

(1) orbit around the Sun

(2) have sufficient mass to be round(ish) in shape

(3) have strong enough gravity to 'clear the neighbourhood' of objects around it.

Pluto goes around the Sun and is round in shape, but there are lots of other objects that orbit alongside it. For that reason, it was reclassified as a dwarf planet, though out of respect for Clyde Tombaugh's work, Pluto is still considered a planet in Illinois, where he was born, and New Mexico, where he lived for many years.

· ·

How can I remember the order of the planets?
There used to be a very clever mnemonic for remembering the planets in order of their distance from the Sun. The first letters of Mercury, Venus, Earth, Mars, Jupiter, Saturn, Uranus, Neptune and Pluto can be recalled using the phrase 'My Very

Easy Method Just Speeds Up Naming Planets'. Since Pluto's relegation, this has been adapted to 'My Very Easy Method Just Seems Useless Now'. But if you want to include Pluto, along with the other dwarf planets – Ceres, Haumea, Makemake and Eris – we can offer: 'My Valiant Elves Made Changes, Just So Underappreciated New Planets Have More Equality.'

· **PLUTONIC FACTS** ·

❯ In 2015, the NASA probe *New Horizons* conducted the first close-up fly-by of Pluto. On board were some of Clyde Tombaugh's ashes, in honour of his discovery of the dwarf planet 85 years earlier.

❯ Most features on Charon, Pluto's moon, are named after famous science-fiction characters and settings. A future spacecraft might land on Gallifrey Macula, Vulcan Planum or Skywalker Crater.

❯ Mike Brown, the astronomer responsible for the reclassification of Pluto, called his memoir *How I Killed Pluto and Why It Had It Coming*.

Is there the same amount of water on Earth as there has always been?

At school we are taught that although water is constantly shape-shifting between ice, liquid and vapour, and moving between oceans, clouds and raindrops, the total amount of it on Earth never changes. However, the truth is that over the past 4 billion years, our planet has lost a quarter of its H_2O.

Water in the clouds gets buffeted by the Sun's rays, which break some of its molecules into their constituent parts, hydrogen and oxygen. Oxygen is heavy enough that it is pulled back down to Earth by gravity, but hydrogen atoms are so light that some of them manage to float away out of the atmosphere and into space. That leaves us with less hydrogen with which to make water, and so the Earth is slowly drying up. At the moment we're losing the equivalent of 50 paddling pools' worth every day.

This process is set to continue, with scientists predicting that Earth will eventually dry out completely. However, since that won't happen for about another billion years, it probably isn't worth getting too worried about.

The bad news is that while Earth isn't going to run out of water anytime soon, it will become increasingly difficult for many of us to access it as climate change continues to alter weather patterns. This is partly because large bodies of snow and ice, such as glaciers, are extremely useful for long-term, reliable water storage, but as the planet warms, these melt, robbing a quarter of the world's population, in regions like the Himalayas and the Andes, of one of their main sources of water.

As climate change makes the movement of water less predictable, we won't be able to exploit it for agricultural and domestic needs as easily as we once could. This means that even though the quantity of water on the planet is set to remain the same for the foreseeable future, humans will increasingly struggle to harness it.

· · · · · · · · · · · · · · · · WELL, WATER WE HAVE HERE? · · · · · · · · · · · · · · · ·

❯ Scientists believe water first arrived on Earth after being spewed out by a particularly energetic type of comet known as a 'hyperactive comet'.

❯ In 2013, geologists tasted water that had been trapped underground, completely untouched, for at least a billion years. They confirmed that it tasted 'terrible'.

❯ Loch Ness holds more fresh water than all of the lakes in England and Wales combined.

❯ The Amazon river has a greater volume and discharge of water than the world's next six biggest rivers combined.

Can you fill up a black hole?

No. A black hole is created when a star gets so massive that it collapses in on itself and tears a hole in space–time. Anything that gets pulled into a black hole just makes it bigger, so don't bother trying.

Is there such a thing as a white hole?

Maybe. Scientists have been thinking about white holes, the opposite of black holes, for a while now. Instead of sucking everything in like a black hole, a white hole would spew objects out into the universe. Unfortunately, they have yet to be observed, but scientists are keeping their eyes peeled.

· THE HOLE TRUTH ·

❯ When Stephen Hawking was asked what you might find inside a black hole, he answered: 'The seven leather-bound volumes of Proust.'

❯ According to some theories, when you fall into a black hole you are stretched apart in a process called 'spaghettification'.

Where can I get the best Internet connection?

In 2007, the fastest Internet in the world belonged to a 75-year-old woman in Sweden called Sigbritt Löthberg. Sigbritt's son, Peter, is a bit of a legendary figure on the World Wide Web. He is responsible for the architecture of much of Europe's Internet and once said that he was 'sent by God to network the planet'.

His mother was not quite so technologically minded. Despite having a 40-gigabit connection, which would have enabled her to download a full movie in HD in just two seconds, Mrs Löthberg said she found that the most useful thing was that the router gave off lots of heat, so she could use it to dry her laundry.

In 2020, such a fast Internet connection is no longer the stuff of science fiction and Swedish laundry rooms. Some countries are starting to offer 'gig-speed' Internet, which can give similarly rapid connection to anyone who is willing to pay a premium.

Today's equivalent of Peter Löthberg is Bill Corcoran, an academic from Melbourne. He and his team have created a new kind of device called a 'micro-comb', which, they say, gives them unprecedented Internet speed. It works by creating a tiny rainbow of lasers, with each colour sending a different piece of data from one place to another. It can give an Internet speed of 44.2 terabits per second. The Australian experiment could allow you to download every Hollywood movie made in 2019 in under a second. The only drawback is that it won't be able to help with your laundry.

How can I live for ever?

Over 2,200 years ago, Qin Shi Huang became the first emperor of a unified China when he conquered the regions of Zhao, Yan, Wei, Han, Chu and Qi (no relation to us). But the enemy he wanted to defeat most of all was death. The emperor took all sorts of potions and concoctions, including mercury pills, in his attempt to live for ever. Unfortunately, the pills had the opposite effect and he died in 210 BC, probably from mercury poisoning. He was one of at least five emperors of the Tang dynasty to accidentally kill themselves while trying to achieve immortality.

Two of the emperors killed by an elixir of life had previously executed the alchemists who finished off their fathers with other potions of immortality. Nobody is quite sure why the emperors kept falling for the scam: it could have been that the potions made you feel healthy initially (before they killed you); or it could have been that their predecessors' corpses didn't decompose due to the high levels of lead and mercury, which might have convinced them there was something in it.

Modern scientists are still working on a cure for death, and the secret may lie in our telomeres. These are small sequences of genetic information that sit on the tips of chromosomes and help to protect our DNA – like the plastic bits on the ends of shoelaces. Every time a cell divides, the telomere becomes a bit shorter, until the cell can no longer reproduce healthily. Scientists think that if they can lengthen these telomeres, our cells might be able to stay young for ever.

For really good advice on longevity we should turn to an expert, and no one was more qualified than Bob Weighton, who lived to be 112 years old and was England's oldest man for a time. His top tip for a long life was to 'avoid dying'.

. . . .

Can any animals live for ever?

Turritopsis dohrnii, better known as the immortal jellyfish, can go from adulthood back to childhood and, in theory, keep doing it for ever. This doesn't happen in the wild, sadly, as they usually end up getting eaten or dying from disease.

. . . . ETERNAL TRUTHS . . . .

▷ In the 1800s, Leonard 'Live Forever' Jones ran for president of the United States, on a platform of promoting immortality. He took part in every election from 1848 to 1868, when he died of pneumonia.

▷ In 2008, the French village of Sarpourenx had a lack of cemetery space, so it banned its residents from being buried there. The mayor announced that 'offenders would be severely punished'.

Credits

Foreword
Zoe Ball

Editors-in-Chief
Anne Miller
James Harkin
James Rawson

QI Elves
Alex Bell
Jack Chambers
Mandy Fenton
Emily Jupitus
Coco Lloyd
Lydia Mizon
Andrew Hunter Murray
Anna Ptaszynski
Ethan Ruparelia
Dan Schreiber
Liz Townsend
Mike Turner

Executive Editor
Sarah Lloyd

Illustration
Emily Jupitus

Design
Chris Shamwana

Publisher
Laura Hassan

Project Editor
Anne Owen

Editorial Assistant
Mo Hafeez

Copy-Editor and Typesetter
Ian Bahrami

Proofreader
Sarah Barlow

Indexer
Mark Bolland

Art Direction
Donna Payne
Paddy Fox

Production
Pedro Nelson
Jude Gates

Publicity
Rachel Alexander
Ruth Killick
Josh Smith
and Gaby Jerrard for QI

Marketing
John Grindrod

Sales
Sara Talbot
Dave Woodhouse
Mallory Ladd

Audio
Catherine Daly

Legal
Suzanne King

Rights
Lizzie Bishop
Emma Cheshire

With Special Thanks to
John Lloyd, Piers Fletcher and Justin Pollard at QI

Graham Albans, Ellie Caddell, Fiona Day, Merrily Grout,
Hana Lockier, Ricky Marshall, Katie Pollard, James Santer,
Chloe Taylor, Helen Thomas, Mark Waring and Joanna
Wilsher at the BBC

Meryl Hoffman and Callum Fosberry for Zoe Ball

Design Credits
LEGO bricks by LEGO Group and Ole Kirk Kristiansen

Scrabble by Hasbro

Song Credits
'What's Going On?' (performed by Marvin Gaye)
Writers: Al Cleveland, Renaldo Benson, Marvin Gaye

'How Will I Know?' (performed by Whitney Houston)
Writers: George Merrill, Shannon Rubicam, Narada Michael
Walden

'Why Do Fools Fall in Love?' (originally performed by Frankie
Lymon and the Teenagers, covered by Diana Ross)
Writers: Frankie Lymon, Morris Levy, Herman Santiago,
Jimmy Merchant

'What's the Frequency, Kenneth?' (performed by REM)
Writers: Bill Berry, Peter Buck, Mike Mills, Michael Stipe

'What's New Pussycat?' (performed by Tom Jones)
Writers: Burt Bacharach, Hal David

'Life on Mars?' (performed by David Bowie)
Writer: David Bowie

Index

eggs, 100, 125, 134
Egypt, ancient
    afterlife, 180
    baldness cures, 187
    names of, 38–9
    pizza, early, 14
    sundials, 177
    writing, 32
Eiffel Tower, 163
Einstein, Albert, 93, 141
Eleanor of Castile, 149
electrolasers, 82
electrons, 170, 180
elephants, 98–9, 145, 171, 195
Elizabeth II, Queen, 103, 148,
    183
Ellis, Dr Geoff, 140
Emirates (airline), 70
emojis, 35
England
    Civil War, 57, 149
    Ethelred's rule, 40
    in French esteem, 104
    lowest temperature, 50–1
    luncheon, 116
    numbering monarchs, 41
    oldest man, 215
envelopes, 169
enzymes, 122
equator, 205
Erik XIV, King of Sweden, 42
Escobar, Pablo, 8
Essex, 46
Estonia, 61
Ethelred the Unready, 40
European Union, 16, 17, 151, 183
executions, 7, 57, 214
extraterrestrials, 12, 180
eyebrows, 190

eyes, 87, 119, 189
Eystein the Fart, 40

fairs, 127
farts, 19, 132, 133
feathers, 135
feet, soles of, 58–9
Ferrari 250, 148
ferrets, 83
fine structure constant, 180
Finland, 34
First World War, 45
fish, 85, 88–9, 143
flamingos, 47, 98
Flavorlopes, 169
flavouring
    peppermint, 169
    spearmint, 169
flies, 86–7
flitches, 124
flooding, 102
flowers, 26–7, 69
Fogarty, Valentine, 191
Foley, Larry, 94–5
follicles, 186, 187, 190
food
    airline, 71
    biting, 126
    cats', 131
    ducks', 102
    fatty, 15
    grass as, 171
    on ISS, 75, 77
    and longevity, 125
    meals, number of, 116–17
    and plants, 64
    sweet-and-salty, 105
    and tin foil, 170
football, 91, 110, 175

Ford, Henry, 110
Formosa, Argentina, 3
France
    alcohol laws, 117
    'bee's knees' equivalent, 35
    biscuits and sweets, 104, 105,
        106–7
    British passports, 183
    dad jokes, 13
    politicians' seating, 127
    sign language, 156
    wine, 18, 19
Franklin, Benjamin, 33
Frederick the Great, 99
French Revolution, 111
Friday the 13th, 181
friend, man's best, 99
Frozen (film), 37
fruit flies, 87
Fuglesang, Christer, 77
fungi, 64, 66, 122

'gaff' (word), 127
galanin, 15
Game of Thrones (TV series),
    37, 46
Ganymede (moon), 206
gardening, 20
Garland, Judy, 145
garlic breath, 196
Garway, Thomas, 114
gas, natural, 139
geese, 83, 85, 187
genetics, 20, 145, 190, 214
Genghis Khan, 44
George VI, King, 114–15
Germany, 42, 61, 162, 163, 172,
    188
Gestetner, David, 191

Gestuno (sign language), 156
giraffes, 65
glaciers, 210
glass-making, 18–19
glue, 139, 169; *see also*
    superglue
goats, 99
Godiva, Lady, 57
golf balls, 129
Google, 99, 149
goosebumps, 84
'Gordon Bennett', *see* Bennett Jr,
    James Gordon
Grammys, 161
grapefruit, 120–1
grapes, 20, 120, 121
grass, 27, 65, 171
'grass' (rhyming slang), 132
gravity
    asteroids and moons, 206
    and baldness, 187
    and birds' swallowing, 133
    and helium balloons, 78
    planet, definition of, 208
    planet formation, 204
    Pluto, discovery of, 207
    seeds' growth, 68, 69
    Sun, 10
    and water in clouds, 210
Great Dunmow, Essex, 124
Greater London Council, 90
Greece, ancient
    and alphabet, 33
    derivations, 23, 33, 128
    donkeys' feet, eating, 192
    and Egypt's name, 39
    'It's all Greek to me', 34
    non-stick pans, 168
    pizza, early, 14

Old English derivations, 40, 122, 145, 161, 171, 172
Olympic Games, 176
Ontario, 14
orange juice, 118
orchids, 65
Ordulf, Earl of Devon, 130
Orff, Carl: *Schulwerk*, 60, 61
Orwell, George: 'A Nice Cup of Tea', 114
ovaries, 199
overbite, 126
'overwhelmed' (word), 49
owls, 83, 92, 201
Oxford English Dictionary, 87
Oxford University, 176
oxygen, 210
'oxyphenbutazone' (word), 53

Pacific Ocean, 4
Panopoulos, Sam, 14
Parkes, Alexander, 128
Parkesine, 128, 129
passports, 183
patents, 5, 123, 128, 178, 191
peas, 65
peat, 23
Peeping Tom, 57
penguins, 47, 135
penicillin, 122
pepperoni, 15
Pepsi, 77, 105, 165
Persians, 108
petits fours, 107
Petrella, Bob, 174
Phelps, Michael, 88
Phoenicians, 32–3
phones, touch-screen, 93
photosynthesis, 26–7

Picasso, Pablo, 157
pigeons, 47
pigs, 51
pillow menus, 109
pineapple, 14
pints, 16–17
pirates, 152
pizza, 14–15, 118, 139
Planck's constant, 180
planets
    definition, 207–8
    mnemonics, 208–9
    roundness of, 204–5
    stars steal, 206
plants
    communication, 64–5, 66
    custard vs mustard, 21
    detecting damage, 65
    growing, 20, 68–9
    photosynthesis, 26–7
    providing gaps, 66
plastic, 128–9, 139, 168
ploonets, 206
Plunkett, Roy, 168
Pluto (dwarf planet), 207–8, 209
Poland, 42, 161, 183
Polaris (star), 12
poles, 205
polka (dance), 160, 161
polka dots, 160
Polka Tulk Blues Band, 161
Polka-Dot Man, 161
Pollock, Jackson, 158
Polyester (film), 139
polytetrafluoroethylene (PTFE), 168
Ponce de León, Dom Pedro, 155–6
poo, 133, 136, 139, 187, 197

pop music, 164
porcupine quills, boiled, 187
porpoises, 103
Portugal, 34
practising, 157
pregnancy, 193–4
Pridmore, Ben, 174–5
Pringles, 105
Proust, Marcel, 212
Prussia, 99, 159
psocids ('booklice'), 166
Ptah (god), 39
pufferfish, 89
Purcell, Henry, 60

'qi' (word), 53
Qiaotou, China, 93
Qin Shi Huang, 214
quarantine, 137
quartz, 185

rabbits, 200–1
radio, 91
Ragnar Hairy Breeches, King, 42
rain, 79
raisins, 20
rashers, 124
'raspberry tart' (rhyming slang), 132
rats, 195, 201
ravens, 99
reading, 31, 176
recorder (instrument), 60–1
recycling, 67
red, 146–7
reminiscence bump, 164
rhinos, 8, 51
rhyming slang, 132

'right wing' (term), 127
right-handedness, 145, 176
rings, growth, 89
Ritchie, Douglas, 162
rivers, 211
rockets, 73–4
rocks, 44–5, 151
Rome, ancient
    calendar fix, 184
    catapults, 45
    horseshoes, 192
    'horn', no word for, 8
    midday meal, 116
    months, 111
    seedless grapes, 20
    see also Latin derivations
Roosevelt, Franklin D., 115, 181
Ross, Sandy, 94
Royal Dockyards, 22
Royal Mint, 183
Royal Swan Markers, 103
Royal Veterinary College, 85
rubies, 79
'run' (word), 87
running, 176, 201
Russia, 2, 74

Sagres, Portugal, 150
Saint Monday, 110, 111
saliva, 113
salt, 105, 135
salted caramel, 105
San Francisco, 37, 50
sandboys, 95
sapphires, 79
Sargasso Sea, 4
Sarpourenx, France, 215
satellites, 37
Saturn, 205, 206